MW01602142

Prairie Pioneer:
The Life & Times of
Judge Bazel Harrison

Bazel Harrison - the first white settler and the first judge of Kalamazoo County. Portrait painted by Mr. Pardee of Auburn, New York. (courtesy Western Michigan University Archives and History Collection.)

Prairie Pioneer:
The Life & Times of
Judge Bazel Harrison

by

Mary Crose

The Priscilla Press
Allegan Forest, Michigan
1994

Please direct any questions or comments concerning this publication to:
Mary Crose
1400 N. Drake Rd. #162
Kalamazoo, MI. 49006-1966

The cover illustration is a portion of an c. 1850 painting by Kalamazoo pioneer Anthony Cooley. Judge Harrison is seated at the bench in the middle. The painting is reproduced through the courtesy of the Kalamazoo Public Museum.

Title Graphic by Devon Blackwood

ISBN 0-9626408-9-1

First Edition - June 1994

DEDICATION

This book is dedicated

to the residents

and

to the employees of

Friendship Village in Kalamazoo, Michigan,

who greatly encouraged the author through

the many hours of research and writing.

ACKNOWLEDGEMENTS

Special thanks are due to the those who provided valuable information, documents, photographs and encouragement during these many months that this book has been in the making. For assistance in gathering information, I sincerely thank:

Virginia Handy of the Michigan Log Cabin Society

Kalamazoo Friendship Village residents and staff for the interest and encouragement shown while this book was in preparation and for the historical materials available in the library

Kalamazoo Gazette for its research and publication of numerous articles relating to the Harrison family

Kalamazoo Nature Center

Kalamazoo Public Library staff for assistance in locating historical documents

Kalamazoo Public Museum and its former curator Alexis Praus, who was responsible for the archeological finding of artifacts on the site of the Harrison log cabin

Steve Lord

Len and Dolly Polson

Mr. and Mrs. Will Redding

Jack Shoemaker

Mary Jane Swartz, author of *So I'm Told*

Dr. Charles VanRiper, retired Western Michigan University professor and author

Nancy Welsh, owner of the Schoolcraft home made famous by James Fenimore Cooper and his "Oak Openings"

Western Michigan University Archives and Regional History Collections staff who provided documents and reproductions of historic photographics

Photos Courtesy of:

Colby Log Cabin, Benton Harbor, Michigan
Earl Cramer
Kalamazoo Public Museum
Kalamazoo Nature Center
Kalamazoo Public Library
Museum of Science & Industry, Chicago, Illinois
Len and Dolly Polson
Linda Rinehart
Western Michigan University Archives & History Collection, Kalamazoo Michigan

Models in the photos include:

Becky Sherfield, Portage, Michigan
Julia Sherfield, Portage, Michigan
Mrs. Prigcon, Gobles, Michigan
and the author, Mary Crose

TABLE OF CONTENTS

PREFACE

I have written this story in order that my family that consists of nephews, nieces, "grands" and "greats", may become better acquainted with our ancestor Judge Bazel Harrison. However, I must add that this goes for all of you history buffs who live in Kalamazoo County and beyond. Neither can I forget you who are related to him. I believe there are 450 of you who attended the 150th anniversary of the arrival of Bazel and Martha Harrison on November 8, 1828 at Prairie Ronde.

The *Kalamazoo Gazette* has published many articles pertaining to the life of Bazel Harrison. They began their articles in 1833 and continued until September of 1991, even though Harrison passed away in 1874. Well-known local historians have included him in their writings. James Stone, the proprietor and editor of the *Kalamazoo Telegraph* wrote an article in 1874, the year of Bazel Harrison's death. This was an account of his eventful life of 103 years, beginning with his birth and ending with his funeral, which was attended by about 1,000 people. As far as I know, no one has ever taken the available accumulated research and put it all together in one volume. It is my intent and purpose to do this very thing.

In writing the story, I have used authentic historical facts and embellished them with my own imagination.

The reader will be introduced to a little band of 21 brave pioneers who left the comforts of life to face the frightening and harrowing experiences of traveling a roadless terrain and will observe Mr. Harrison as he demonstrates the unique characteristics which made him truly a great man.

Mary Elizabeth Crose

HARRISON FAMILY TREE

Bazel Harrison   married   Martha Stillwill

Bazel's and Martha's daughter Almira Harrison married John Crose

Almira and John's son was Jesse Crose

Jesse's son was Lloyd Crose.
His children are Mary Crose (the author) and John Crose

John had five children. They are listed below
and their children's names follow

Wilma	Don	Shirley	Jean	Evelyn
James	Pam	Colleen	Larry	Patty
Linda	Robin	Randy	Glenna	Judy
Tom	Greg	Sam	Steve	Karen
Leonard	Sandy			

CHAPTER 1 - HOW IT ALL BEGAN

Clang, clang, clang go the fire trucks as they race down Michigan Avenue. OOOO scream the sirens of an ambulance as it follows the fire trucks. Buses toot their horns as they turn the corner of an intersection to park at a curb. People are hurrying across the street, trying to beat the green light before it turns to yellow. Tall buildings loom to the right, smaller buildings stand at the left. These are the sights and sounds one encounters while making his way along the crowded sidewalks of Kalamazoo.

Now we will get in our car and go to Schoolcraft, about a 25-minute ride from downtown Kalamazoo, to see what life in that village is like. Rather different, we say, since this is a village of about 1300 people. The buildings in Schoolcraft are much smaller than those in Kalamazoo and different sounds are heard on the streets. Big trucks rumbling through the main street can rattle objects off the store shelves. Sometimes it is hard for a clerk to talk to a customer if the rumbling is too loud. Speeding cars also cause noise problems.

Let's go back 150 years and imagine what the villages of Kalamazoo and Schoolcraft were like in those days. They would be quiet. Perhaps you could hear birds chirping and calling to their mates. Indian children might be playing outside their wigwam homes. The Indian mother, called a squaw, might be poking the fire where she is cooking meat in a kettle hanging over the open fire. We might see an Indian brave cutting down saplings and placing them in the ground, bending over the tops, covering them with bark, grass matting or boughs to make a wigwam.

As we think of Kalamazoo and Schoolcraft as quiet places to live, two white men come from the Eastern part of our country to make these two locations their homes. Titus Bronson came to live in Kalamazoo and Bazel Harrison chose to make Schoolcraft his home.

This story tells how Bazel Harrison came to Schoolcraft and the exciting adventures he had during the 103 years of his life. The Harrison family came from a part of the country which was many, many, miles from Schoolcraft and when they came west, they did not find lots of people or cars or houses in the village as we have now. What they did find when they arrived was like the last imaginary picture I told you about: Indians, wigwams and a different way of life than we know today.

Now we are going to climb onto a magic carpet that will take us up in the air all the way to the eastern part of the United States to the state of Maryland where Bazel Harrison was born. This state is near the great big Atlantic Ocean and it was one of the states where there were cities, boats on rivers, schools and houses something like we have today.

Bazel Harrison was born a long, long time

ago -- more than 200 years ago on March 15, 1771. He had 22 brothers and sisters. His father was married twice. The first wife was the mother of some of the 23 children and after she died he married again and the rest of the children, including Bazel, were born.

It must have cost a lot of money to feed and take care of such a large family and as soon as they were old enough the boys had to help on the farm or get work wherever they could. The girls helped their mother keep house.

Bazel was a smart boy, but went to the village school for only three months. He found out that books could give lots of knowledge, so when one of his friends got a new book, Bazel would ask if he could borrow it. He would read it and always return it when he said he would. When he grew older and worked, he bought more books, if he had any money left after paying his father for his room and board.

The family moved from Maryland to Virginia, then to Pennsylvania. Bazel's older brothers and sisters married and only Bazel was left at home with his mother and father and the younger children. During most of his early years,he helped his father on the farm, but when he was 14 years old, he began to work in a distillery. A distillery is a place where alcoholic drinks are made. Even though Bazel worked with beer and whisky, he never drank any of it. He said one of the reasons he lived such a long life was because he drank only milk.

We do not know a great deal about Bazel's early life, but we do know that he was a hard worker, ambitious and whatever he did he did well. He was always a clean boy and kept his clothes patched. He did not like clothes that were dirty or ragged.

Now we are coming to a happy part of the story. Like most young men, Bazel wanted to be married. Down the road from the Harrison family home lived a beautiful 16-year old girl named Martha Stillwell. At this time, Bazel was a mature 19 years old.

Bazel went to see Martha on Saturday when he was not working. He watched this beautiful girl, who was always kind to her family. She was never saucy to her parents, but always obeyed them. She was a good house-keeper and cook. Her mother taught her to use a loom and she made yards and yards of cloth, which she and her mother and sister made into clothes for the family.

Bazel had many of the same good qualities as Martha. He was kind to everyone he met and tried to do nice things for people. He was always obedient to his parents, also. So the two young people had many things in common. Soon Bazel fell in love with this lovely girl. One day he told her how much he loved her and asked her to marry him. "Oh, Bazel," said Martha, "I love you, too, and would like to marry you, but you will have to ask Mother and Father,"

That very night Bazel went to talk to Mr.

Stillwell, who was in the backyard cutting wood for the fireplace. "Mr. Stillwell," said Bazel, "you have such a wonderful daughter. I have come to ask you if I may have her as my wife?"

"Yes, my boy," said Mr. Stillwell. "I have noticed that you have so many fine qualities that I would gladly say yes, yes, yes. You certainly may have my daughter in marriage, but I don't know what her mother will say."

"I am not so sure that she is as willing as I. You see, Bazel," Mr. Stillwell continued, "my wife wants Martha to marry a rich man. Go talk to her and maybe you can win her as you have won me."

Bazel found Dame Stillwell in the loom room weaving yarn into cloth so that she could have a new dress. "Good evening, Dame Stillwell," said Bazel. "This is a nice evening, isn't it?"

"Yes, it is," said Martha's mother.

"You do beautiful weaving," said Bazel. He was finding it hard to ask the question. Finally, Bazel got up enough courage to say in a choking voice, "Dame Stillwell, may I marry your daughter, Martha? I love her very much."

Dame Stillwell became very angry. She said in a loud voice, "The very likes of you to ask such a question. You...you...do you have a beautiful home? do you have lots of money, a big farm? Do you have servants? Or will my daughter have to scrub the floors, wash the dishes and get along on little money? I should say not! You may not have my daughter. I need her to help me with my housework. Leave at once!"

Poor Bazel was very disappointed. He knew that Martha would only be happy with his love and he just could not imagine living without her. Mr. Stillwell was waiting outside the loom room door where he had heard everything his wife said. Bazel came out of the door with tears in his eyes and when he was far enough away so Dame Stillwell could not hear him he said, "I guess we can't get married."

Mr. Stillwell threw is arms around the young man and said, "I know how you feel, Bazel. I am certain that something can be worked out!" After a moment he continued, "I have a plan, we will play a trick on my wife. We will make the wedding plans and she doesn't have to know about it. You are such an honest, upright boy and your parents have brought you up to work hard and to save your money. I cannot let you go. There would never be a better husband for my daughter than you, Bazel Harrison."

So, Mr. Stillwell began to think of a plan. That was it...he would help them elope. Elope means that Bazel and Martha would have a secret wedding and Dame Stillwell would not know about it.

"You know, Bazel," said Mr. Stillwell, "Martha is a good seamstress and I think with the help of her sister, she could make her own wedding dress. They could work on it after their mother goes to bed and she will never know." Martha and her sister worked late into the night until the dress was finished and it was beautiful.

Mr. Stillwell eagerly watched the progress of the dress, but one thing worried him. It was the custom or rule in those days for all brides to wear nice shoes. Martha only had brogans, rough looking leather shoes that she wore outdoors when the weather was cold. Indoors she went barefoot. The family lived far from the big cities where ready-made shoes were purchased. There was a cobbler in a nearby village, but he could not make any shoes without knowing the size of Martha's feet. The wedding was getting closer and Mr. Stillwell had to measure Martha's feet without Dame Stillwell knowing about it.

Finally, another idea popped into his head and he told Bazel about his plan. He would take a shingle into the loom room before Martha and her mother went in to weave. Then he would come into the loom room, would joke about the size of Martha's feet and draw around them on the shingle. Then he would throw the shingle out the window and Bazel would be there to take it to the cobbler. The plan worked perfectly and the cobbler worked far into the night to finish the shoes. They were beautiful dainty pumps with little high heels and looked just perfect with the wedding dress.

The wedding day came and at dinnertime

Martha told her mother that she did not feel like eating. She left the table with her father and ran away to be married. Mr. Stillwell took her to the justice of the peace where Bazel was waiting. Bazel and his beautiful bride were married on March 17, 1790, the beginning of a long and happy marriage.

And what about Mrs. Stillwell? She was suspicious that something strange was going on, but she never asked what it was. When she found that she had been outwitted, she was very angry, but when she realized what a fine young man her daughter had married, she soon got over her anger.

CHAPTER 2 - ELIAS PLANS TO VISIT MICHIGAN

The newly-married Bazel and Martha Harrison began housekeeping in a small house that was not at all like the one Martha's mother wanted her to have. But the young couple thought it was a mansion. Bazel and Martha were very much in love and that love produced a warm and loving family as each new baby arrived.

The Harrisons moved from Maryland to Virginia and remained there until 1810, during which time ten children were born. They were William, Sarah. Nathan, Shadrach, Ephriam, Joseph, Cynthia, Elias, Worlenda, and one infant who died unnamed. Little is known about the Harrison's early married life, except that they had 17 children in all. The younger ones were Bazel,Jr., Martha, Rachel, Amanda, John, Diana and Almira, who was the author's great-grandmother.

In 1810, the large family moved to Kentucky, just opposite Cincinnati. For two years Bazel made a living for his family by distilling. He was now living near his cousin William Henry Harrison, who would later become President of the United States. When the War of 1812 broke out, William Harrison left his farm to fulfill his duties as a commanding officer. Though Bazel was brave, he did not like to fight, so he sent his brother Ephraim to fight in his place. While William Harrison was commanding his forces and could not work his farm, he asked Bazel to work the farm on shares. This way Bazel and his cousin divided whatever money was earned on the farm.

When the war was over, Bazel bought a 300-acre farm of his own about 12 miles from Springfield, Ohio. His oldest, son, William, also bought his own farm. The family lived on the Ohio farm for about ten years and was prosperous. But they heard reports from people who traveled to Michigan and told about the wonderful country there. Bazel's son, Elias, decided that he wanted to see this beautiful county north of Ohio and Indiana and perhaps to settle there.

On a beautiful May day when the green leaves of the maple trees had popped out, the county road was lined with beautiful flowers of blue, pink, white, yellow, purple and red. Bazel was standing near the pig pen throwing ears of field corn to the pigs, when he heard the clop, clop sound of horse's hoofs. A beautiful brown horse came galloping up the drive into the Harrison farm yard. Looking up from the grunting, squealing pigs, Bazel saw his son Elias stop his horse, drop the reins and dismount. Elias was grinning from ear to ear. "Hello," he said, "how do you like him?" pointing to his new friend. "Just bought him from Jim Cole." Jim was a neighbor of the Harrisons. "His name is Brownie and is he ever smart. He knows everything you say to him" continued the excited young man. Brownie began to neigh, "He, he, he, he." He seemed to say, "I like Elias and I know he will be good to me." Then Brownie stamped his feet.

"Oh, Elias," Bazel said, "you have a fine looking horse and I am sure he is everything you say he is. Intelligence is the main thing and I can see he has it." Brownie snorted, stamped his feet again and playfully took a handkerchief out of Bazel's pocket.

"Well, boy," Bazel continued, "you certainly know everything I am saying to you," and he patted Brownie's head.

"Dad," said Elias, "I have come to tell you that Brownie and I are going on a trip."

"Just where are you going?" questioned his father.

"You see, Dad, I hear that Michigan is a territory just waiting to be explored. Brownie and I are going on an adventure. As soon as I can pack what we may need, we will start."

"But, Elias," Bazel asked, "do you realize you are going on a very dangerous journey? There are no white people there. I hear there are only Indians. What would you eat? There are no roads and you might be eaten up by wild animals. Don't go, Elias. I will worry about you."

"Never mind, Dad, my mind is made up."

"Then go, Elias, and may you have devine guidance."

By the next day Elias gathered all the equipment he thought he would need and put it on Brownie's back. The family gathered together to bid him good-bye. There were tears in Martha's eyes as she understood the dangers her son might encounter.

I wonder what Brownie is thinking! Could it be about the time he saved everyone in the camp from being eaten by wolves?

CHAPTER 3 - EXPLORING THE UNKNOWN

"Well, Brownie," said Elias as they started on their perilous journey, "we have made up our minds to see this trip through to the end haven't we?"

"He, he, he," answered Brownie in his special horse language, as if to say, "I won't let you down, Elias."

The day ws warm and both horse and rider enjoyed a gentle breeze. As they travelled through villages and cities, Elias shopped for needed supplies. finally, they reached Fort Wayne, corssed the Indiana border and arrived in southern Michigan.

The trip had not been easy. Sometimes he had to chop down trees in order to make a path through the forest. At night, he tried to find a grassy spot near a lake where Brownie could graze and they could drink water. Elias would unroll the tent that Brownie had carried on his back and after carefully pitching it, woul dhead for the lake to fish for his supper.

The sound of sizzling fish in a frying pan over an open fire whetted Elias' appetite. and soon the aroma of the fish cooking in the pork fat he had brought with him let him know it was nearly dinner time. Brownie was not forgotten. His master had brought food for him to supplement the tender grass they found at the campsites.

Elias kept the fire burning all night to

keep him warm and to frighten off the howling wolves. It was necessry for him to replenish teh wood he had gathered during daylight hours several times each night.

"Brownie," said Elias, "those wolves don't sound good to me. I have my flint lock rifle loaded in case we need it." Before he lay down for the night, he committed himself and Brownie to his Heavenly Guide.

In the morning Elais awoke and enjoyed the sun streaming in the tent door. Brownie had been stirring for sometime and Elias found him enjoying the luscious green grass.

"Good morning, Brownie," said Elias, "I wonder if we will see any Indians today. To tell the truth, I am somewhat frightened to meet them."

CHAPTER 4 - NOISES

Elias had just finished a breakfast of corn meal mush and bacon. Brownie had his fill of oats. Elias started to pack his equipment on Brownie's back. Suddenly the horse stood still. What was that crackling noise that broke the stillness?

Elias and Brownie looked toward a cluster of trees. Coming towrd them were three tall, smiling Indians. They work shirts and trousers made of bright colored cloth. Traveling traders had traded the cloth for animal skins which the Indians had tanned. Before the traders came, the Indians wore clothes made of animal skins.

Walking toward Elias and Brownie, one Indian, who appeared to be the chief, stretched out his hand. He grasped Elias' hand with ahearty shake. As he did so he said in English, "White man welcome!" He then pointed to Brownie saying "horse." Elias was very startled to hear these English words. Later he learned about some traders who had visited these Indians and had taught them some English words.

Chief Ref Feather beckoned to Elias to follow him.

Some Indians lived in tepees which were easily rolled up and taken to new locations as they moved from place to place.

CHAPTER 5 - MAKING NEW FRIENDS

Chief Red Feather headed the procession as it wended its way along the narrow path, bordered by trees.

Suddenly the chief stopped, then led the party through an opening. What a peaceful picture met Elias' eyes. Indian children were playing and laughing. An Indian squaw was leaning over a black kettle, which was attached to three sticks that made a tripod. She was stirring venison stew.

"Whatever is cooking in the pot sure smells good," Elias thought. "I haven't had meat since I left home." He heard voices and saw two men building a wigwam from young sapling branches. You see, these Indians lived in wigwams instead of tepees.

Red Feather took Elias' arm and led him to the Indian squaw and introduced him to her. He told Red Feather his name, so he didn't have to just be called "White Man." When the squaw saw Elias she stood up. Smiling, she held out her hand for him to shake and said, "Hungry? We eat." As Elias was introduced to the other Indian braves, he learned they also knew some English words.

White Dove, the Indian squaw brought out some clay dishes. The children were called and everyone sat down on the ground cross-legged to enjoy the delicious stew. The Indians laughed, gestured and conversed with Elias using the

English words they knew. He explained that he wanted to learn the Potawatomi language.

In the meantime, Brownie spied three Indian ponies grazing nearby. Galloping over to them, he introduced himself in horse language. Soon they were neighing, and shinnying as if they were old friends. All four began to gallop around a grassy opening. After a good workout they returned to their masters. Brownie must have thought to himself, "Now I have Indian friends, too."

I wonder if Elias will learn some Indian words. Let's read in the next chapter how he went to Indian School.

Tepee - Siouan: A cone shaped tent used by American Indians. Also spelled teepee.

Wigwam - Algonquin: A conical shelter made by Indians of eastern and central North America, consisting of poles covered with bark, hides, etc.

The Potawatomi Indians from southwest Michigan lived in wigwams made by first creating frames from young saplings as shown in this photo taken at the Kalamazoo Nature Center.

The wigwam frames were covered with bark to create shelter from the weather.

CHAPTER 6 - ELIAS GOES TO SCHOOL

The next day the friends started their language classes. Elias wanted to learn Potawatomi words and his Indian friends wanted to know more English than they had a chance to learn from the traders. They used objects; they acted out words; they painted pictures on animal skins. Soon they were talking to each other. Elias learned quickly. When it was time to leave his friends to return to Ohio, he knew a number of Potawatomi words.

He met other Indians of the same tribe who traveled from about 40 miles north. They told him about a lake and a prairie. They said, "There is grass which is so high that when the wind blows it looks likes the waves on a lake. The soil is black and fertile. Vegetables grow well and beautiful flowers of all colors make the landscape a beautiful place to behold. The corn grows higher than a tall man."

Elias explored the countryside. He helped the Indians hunt, fish, make wigwams and he learned about Indian ways. He played with the children; he taught them English words. In fact, everyone loved him so much, it was a sad day when his visit ended.

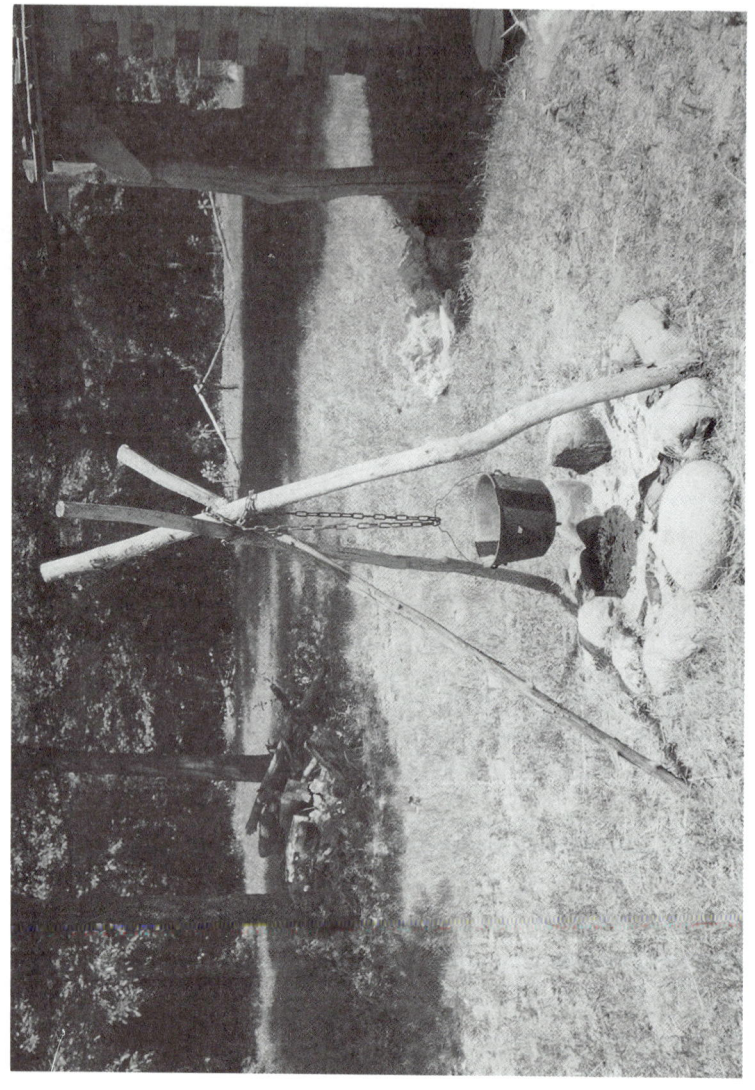

When Elias visited Michigan, he saw the Indians cooking their stew in a kettle hung on a tripod over an open fire.

CHAPTER 7 - THE EXPLORERS SAY GOODBYE

It was August 27th, 1827. Elias must return to his family which he had left in Ohio. It was an unhappy day as the dear friends he loved gathered to say "goodbye." As he left the little group, he said, "Perhaps we shall see each other again."

Little did he know then what exciting events would take place in the fall of 1828 or how important his knowledge of the Indian language would mean to him.

As the galloping horse rode away, Elias turned around several times to wave goodbye.

The trip home was much easier than when he had come because he remembered the obstacles which had confronted him and now he could avoid them.

Brownie was carrying supplies provided by the Indians which would last him until he reached the cities and villages where he could purchase more.

The time went fast and soon they were nearing home. Brownie was happy to know he would soon be seeing his beloved family. It seemed as if his legs just flew over the road.

CHAPTER 8 - HOME AGAIN

After a breathtaking experience of holding tightly to Brownie's reins, Elias rode into the Harrison driveway. He made the trip in two weeks. The dogs were there to greet the travelers, barking their loudest and jumping all over Elias, but as soon as they heard his commanding voice to be still, they obeyed. They all had their share of patting and affection from their kind master. Brownie was so excited he began to neigh and paw the ground. Mr. Harrison emerged from the barn and ran with youthful agility across the yard to greet his son.

When Mrs. Harrison and the children heard Brownie neighing and stomping his feet, they realized the son and big brother was home. Out the back door they ran pell-mell into the yard where pandemonium reigned! Everyone was talking at once as they smothered Elias with their hugs and kisses. Oh, yes, they didn't forget Brownie either. He also had his share of attention.

John began shouting, "Elias, tell us all about Michigan!"

"Yes, do," said 13-year old Martha, "we can't wait to hear about your trip."

"Oh! yes you can," said Elias. "We haven't eaten anything since yesterday. We were so anxious to get home we just came non-stop, didn't we, Brownie?" Brownie shook his head and said, "He, he, he!"

"Oh! you blessed dears," exclaimed Mother Harrison. "Dad, give Brownie his dinner, then all of you come into the house. I have lunch ready. After we eat we will give Elias a chance to answer our questions. I want to know all bout Michigan too."

The children ran to the house and were soon seated at the table. What did they have to eat? You guessed it! Of course, there was a great big platter of friend corn meal mush, everyone' favorite. Mother knew how to fry it so it was crisp and delicious. Butter and syrup made it extra tasty.

After father Harrison thanked God for Elias' and Brownie's safe trip, a lively conversation followed. Each member of the family was thinking about the question he or she planned to ask.

When everyone had finished eating, Elias said, "Thank you, Mother for this good home cooking. There is nothing like it."

"You are welcome," said Mother Harrison. "it is good to have you back. Now let's all go into the living room and Elias will tell us all about Michigan."

CHAPTER 9 - ELIAS ANSWERS QUESTIONS

The family moved into the living room and after each member was seated, Elias asked, "Who wants to start the questions?"

"I do," said Bazel Junior. "Does corn grow in Michigan?"

"It certainly does and I heard from the Indians who live about 40 miles north of the Indiana border, that it grows very tall," answered Elias.

"I would love to see it," said the farmer-minded Bazel Junior.

"What about Indians?" asked eight-year old John. "Do they fight white people?"

"No, no, these Indians are friendly and only fight among themselves," Elias responded. "I lived with them for a while and we became the best of friends. They even taught me some Indian words. They belong to the Potawatomi tribe. Who else has a questions?" asked Elias.

"I do," responded 17-year old Worlenda. "I have heard there are wolves in Michigan. Did you see any?"

"No," said Elias, "I didn't see any, but I certainly heard them. Sometimes it was hard to sleep because they howled so loudly, but I kept a big bonfire burning all night. Wolves do not like fire, so they stayed away. I also had my flint lock rifle handy. If they had come near me in the daytime, they would have been dead wolves."

Question after question was asked. Everyone agreed that Michigan must be a land of opportunity. Father Harrison was very impressed with Elias' glowing report. It started him thinking about taking his family and settling in this territory.

The pioneers cooked outdoors over a tripod just as the Indians did. During the summer, this method of cooking prevented the cabins from heating up. This, and many of the pictures used to illustrate this book, were taken at the Bee Hive Farm in Gobles, Michigan.

CHAPTER 10 - A MILITARY MESSAGE

A year had quickly passed since Elias had returned from Michigan. Bazel Harrison and his sons had worked hard that summer. The crops were good. The garden was full of vegetables: carrots, onions, potatoes and cabbage. The corn was especially good this season. Apple trees were loaded with the red juicy fruit. There was plenty of food to last all fall and winter and into the spring. Neighbors had helped with the harvesting.

Mr. Harrison had risen early that morning and with the help of Elias and eight-year-old John, had milked the cows, Flossie, LulaBelle and Ginger.

Mother Harrison had prepared a good breakfast of fried corn meal mush. Just as everyone had finished eating, there was a commotion in the drive. The dogs were barking as was their habit when a visitor arrived. Mr. Harrison went to the back door and saw a man on a galloping horse. He left the house in order to greet the visitor.

"Be quiet, dogs. Stop your barking!" he commanded. The man stopped his horse and jumped off. Mr. Harrison noticed that he was wearing a badge.

"Are your Bazel Harrison?" the man inquired.

"Yes, I guess I happen to be the person you are looking for. Just what is your business?" he questioned.

"Mr. Harrison, here are some papers which I am delivering to you from the United States Army," responded the man who was wearing a military uniform.

"My name is Green, Alger Green."

"How do you do, Mr. Green," said Father Harrison and gave him a hearty hand shake. "Come in the house and my wife will fry some of her delicious corn meal mush. You must be hungry."

Mother Harrison was clearing the tables. "Martha," said Father Harrison. "I want you to meet Mr. Green." Mrs. Harrison gave him a great big smile as she shook his hand.

"Martha," he said, "would you please give Mr. Green some of your fried corn meal mush? He can eat it while I read some papers which he delivered to me."

"I certainly appreciate our kindness," said Mr. Green. "You see, I left home at 5 o'clock this morning and I didn't want to bother my wife to prepare breakfast. Does that mush ever smell and look good. I am just starved." He ate piece after piece.

While Mother Harrison and Mr. Green were carrying on a lively conversation, Father Harrison read the papers. What did they say? As he read them, he began to frown.

CHAPTER 11 - UPSETTING NEWS

"Oh, Bazel," said Martha, "something terrible has happened, has it not?" I can tell from the expression on your face.

"Yes, Martha, it has happened again," said Father Harrison. "Do you remember when General William Henry Harrison went in 1812 to command troops for the United States Army?"

"I certainly do," said Mrs. Harrison. "I remember how we moved onto his farm and you worked it on shares. You also paid your brother Ephraim to go to war in your place."

"That's right, Martha. You also remember the army told us we would have to give up our farm to a soldier who did go to war. Instead of giving it away, we gave him $700. You also know the army asked us to do this three times so far and this will make the fourth time we are paying for it. We have done well in a financial way. In spite of losing $2,800, we have been able to save a considerable sum. There is no telling how many times the army will expect us to repeat this transaction."

"That's right," said Mrs. Harrison.

"Since Elias visited Michigan, I have been thinking a great deal about selling some of our stock, farm equipment and household goods. We could then move up there," replied Mr. Harrison.

"I heartily agree with you, dear husband, I know it won't be easy, but we cannot continue giving away our money," commented Mother Harrison.

What an enormous problem faced the Harrison family. What will they do about it?

Artists of the mid 19th century drew strange looking sheep.

CHAPTER 12 - A BIG DECISION

The day after Mr. Green's visit, Mr. Harrison fully made up his mind to "Go West." However, he knew Michigan was really northwest of Ohio.

After breakfast, he called the family together to announce his plan. After everyone was quiet, Mr. Harrison began, "Today is a very important one in our lives. You see, dear ones, Mr. Green, who visited us, gave me some very bad news. He came to tell me that because I did not go to war, I now must give my farm to a man who did go or pay him $700. I have already paid $2,100 to three other men and if I keep this farm this time, I will be paying out $2,800 in all.

"Your mother and I have talked it over and we have decided to let the last man have the farm. We will sell much of our farm equipment and furniture and live stock. We will then travel to Michigan. This move will not be easy. Our legs and feet will become weary as we will have to do a great deal of walking. I want to take about 50 of our sheep and an equal number of hogs, in addition to the horses and three cows. They will have to walk all of the way and with the help of the dogs, we will take turns guiding them.

"It will be necessary to cut down trees in order to travel where there are no roads. Since we will be doing something which no others in this part of the country have tried, I am sure we will have many discouraging moments. It will be more difficult for us to travel than it was for Elias as he had only Brownie and we will have to clear spaces for the wagons and animals to go through.

"I am going to Springfield tomorrow to purchase a Conestoga wagon. Do you know anything about this kind of a vehicle?"

"I don't," said 14-year old Bazel Junior.

"I don't," said Martha. "Dad, tell us about one," she continued.

Mr. Harrison began. "It is a large wagon which has a white canvas cover. The body is painted blue. We will use it to carry our furniture and farm equipment; that is, what we have left after our sale.

"When we arrive in Michigan, there will be no white people and no stores where we can purchase any of these things. We will have to take enough food to last us through the fall and winter. We will have to live off the land by hunting and fishing. Elias says there is a lake on a prairie. I hope to settle there. We can also fish through the ice in the winter.

"In the summer we can farm and grow vegetables, so we should have no problem regarding food. The Conestoga will be pulled by four horses. The one I want is very large. Of course, we will be taking some smaller covered wagons, too.

"I can just see us fishing from the shore. After we have enough, we can build a fire and fry the fish right there by the water's edge. Just imagine us turning those sizzling light brown bass. Oh, won't they taste good along with mother's delicious bread?

"I trust tomorrow will be a beautiful day for my trip to Springfield. I shall make arrangements with Elias to borrow Brownie."

Will Mr. Harrison find a used Conestoga? Let's read on and see.

Conestoga wagons carried many pioneers westward.

CHAPTER 13 - SPRINGFIELD, HERE WE COME

Elias was in the garden digging potatoes. When he heard someone walking toward him, he looked up. "Hello, Dad, aren't these potatoes beautiful? Our crops are the best we've ever had."

"They certainly are," answered his father. "Just seems as if everything is coming our way. We are going to need every potato we have grown to take to Michigan. In fact, the crops are very abundant. I feel something like the pilgrims must have felt during their first year in America. The one big difference is they had completed their year of hardships and we are just beginning ours. But, they had great faith in God. We must be brave in tackling our great venture. We too, can look to the same One for guidance and the wisdom we are going to need to see this trip through.

"I have come to ask you a favor, Elias. May I borrow Brownie tomorrow? I will need him to ride to Springfield. I trust I can find a used Conestoga."

"You certainly may, Dad. I will have him ready any time you say."

"I should start as early as possible. Let's say about eight-thirty," Bazel replied.

The next day dawned bright and clear. Mr. Harrison ate a hearty breakfast as he knew it would take him most of the day to complete his mission. Mother Harrison had risen early and made fresh home made bread especially for her dear husband.

The aroma of the bread filled the whole house. As he came into the kitchen, he said, "Martha, you make the best bread I have ever tasted." He went to the cool basement where food was kept. You see, there were no freezers or refrigerators in 1828. He brought up several pieces of ham and made sandwiches to take with him.

Just then, he heard, "he, he, he." Mr. Harrison kissed his wife goodbye. Then he went to each of his children and kissed them goodbye, too. Each had a big hug, also. Then he went out to the waiting Brownie.

Father Harrison, at the age of 57, was tall, strong and handsome. He could be stern, but he was very kind. All of his children adored him and obeyed his every command. They trusted him completely and knew that whatever he said, or did, was for their good.

Punishment was rarely meted out. There was no need for it. Of course, Mrs. Harrison had the same respect from the children. If ever a household ran smoothly, it was that of the Harrison's!

Mr. Harrison, with great agility, put his foot in the stirrup which hung down from Brownie's side. He threw his other foot over the horse's back and fit it into the other stirrup. As horse and rider drove out of the yard and on to the main road, many hands were waving "good-bye."

This illustration from an 1873 edition of Cooper's *Oak Openings* shows the wedding of the Bee Hunter and Margery.

CHAPTER 14 - BROWNIE MAKES A NEW FRIEND

Everyone ran to the road and watched Mr. Harrison and Brownie as long as they were visible. Finally, all that could be seen was a small cloud of dust.

The day was warm, but very pleasant. Mr. Harrison enjoyed the cool breeze as it touched his face. Flowers blended into a mass of different hues, yellow, pink, blue and purple. He began to wonder if Michigan would have scenery as beautiful as that in Ohio, a state he had learned to love.

As his body went up and down in tune with the rhythm of Brownie's galloping, he began to talk to him, "You know, boy," he said, "we are going to go on a long journey and we want you to go with us. You are one of us and we love you. We also need you, Brownie, as you are our only riding horse. You are smart and I think we will put you at the head of our cavalcade. You will be our lookout man and I know we can depend on you to detect any danger that lies ahead."

Little did Mr. Harrison realize how much danger they would run into and how useful Brownie would be.

"He, he, he," he said, as if he knew everything his master was saying to him.

After riding about 25 miles, farms began to appear along the road. "I believe, Brownie, we are coming to Springfield." Soon they came to houses which had no farms, but looked as if they were part of a town. They rode a little farther and stores appeared. They passed a grocery store, a bank, a cobbler shop, a black-smith shop and there was a store with a sign, "FARM WAGONS FOR SALE."

Mr. Harrison said, "Whoa, Brownie, I will tie you to this hitching post." He gingerly jumped off the horse and tied him to the post.

In the next chapter, you will learn how Mr. Harrison finds some answers to his questions about Michigan.

CHAPTER 15 - NEWS FROM THE NORTH

As Mr. Harrison walked into the wagon store, he could hear voices which belonged to two men dressed as if they had been on a long journey. He walked over to them and said, "I believe I heard one of you mention Michigan. Is that correct?"

"It certainly is. We have just returned from an exploring and hunting trip. We took some time off from our work to do some traveling up there. We were very curious about this part of our county and wished to satisfy our curiosity," said the taller man.

"Good, good, you are just the persons to whom I would like to address some questions. My name is Bazel Harrison and I live about 25 miles north of this town of Springfield. I am planning to move my family to Michigan and I know absolutely nothing about this territory, except what my son has told me. You see, a year ago he rode up there on horseback, visited some Indians and did some exploring. I am here today to purchase a used Conestoga."

"I think we can answer some of your questions, Mr. Harrison. My name is Jim White and my friend here is Tom Manning."

"I am glad to meet both of you," said Mr. Harrison as he shook their hands. "Please tell me everything you can about Michigan in the short time we have together."

"No doubt you already know, Mr.Harrison,

that most of southern Michigan is wide open to settlement. Your son probably has told you many things about it which would make you desire to move your family up there. It has many trees which are just waiting to have someone cut them down. They are excellent for use in the construction of houses and other buildings. The forests have openings which look like parks. There are many lakes, streams and rivers which are teeming with fish.

"Many are navigable and would provide opportunities for transporting goods from one place to another. The friendly Indians have no trouble growing crops. Since there are so few settlers, you could just about choose any spot you wish. It has every opportunity which you will need to prosper.

"The government won't be able to take your property to give to someone else, which I hear is happening right here in Ohio. I believe it is possible for one to lose his farm if he did not participate in the war of 1812. His property would be given to another man who did fight. Ohio is becoming a very crowded state."

"By all means, move your family up there. You will never regret it," spoke up Tom Manning. "I agree with everything Jim has said. I could tell you more, but perhaps this much will give you some inspiration. It won't be easy, I warn you. After you leave Fort Wayne, there will be few roads and finally you will come to a place where the roads end. There will be only Indian trails. You will have to chop down trees in order to make a wide enough path to accommodate your wagons.

"But, I must say, Mr. Harrison, you look strong and courageous. I believe you have what it takes to conquer the unknown. I know you will make it. We must go now, but we wish you great success."

"Thank you, Tom and Jim. You have given me new courage to tackle our new venture. If you ever make another trip, look us up," were Mr. Harrison's departing words. With great admiration for this brave man, Tom and Jim left the store, mounted their horses and rode away.

Mr. Harrison watched them as far as he could see the dust that was kicked up by the galloping horses' hoofs. He wondered about the Conestoga and what a big undertaking it would be to sell most of his possessions and to leave his prosperous farm.

He had heard about Conestogas from hunters who were traveling from the East to engage in the lucrative fur business in the Northern part of Michigan.

Just then, he heard a voice from behind him, which interrupted his thoughts. "My name is Max Sheldon. May I help you?" came the words from a salesman who had just finished with a customer.

Will Mr. Harrison find the right kind of a Conestoga? Let us read the next chapter and see.

CHAPTER 16 - THE CONESTOGA

"Yes, you certainly may help me. I am looking for a used Conestoga. You see, I am moving my family to Michigan in a few days and I will need one to carry the farm implements and furniture which we will be taking. We are selling some of it and plan to take only what we will really need," replied Mr. Harrison.

"I think I might have one which would exactly fit your needs. It is a used one and requires four horses to draw it. You know some of the Conestogas are so large they require six or eight horses. This particular kind is used in the East to transport freight from one state to another," commented Mr. Sheldon.

"We have had a good summer as far as the crops are concerned. We must take enough food to last through the fall and all winter, until we can plant our seeds in the spring. With hunting and fishing to supplement, I feel we can make our supplies last," said Mr. Harrison.

"I am sure you are looking ahead at the problems which may arise and you will conquer them," predicted Mr. Sheldon.

"We are taking 50 sheep and 50 hogs, which will be an excellent source of meat," added Mr. Harrison.

"Now coming to the Conestoga, I have a used one which came in yesterday. Let's go outdoors and look at it."

The two men walked through the door and

entered the back yard. There standing in front of them was a beautiful wagon. The body was freshly painted a bright blue and covering it was a clean white canvas.

"Oh, Mr. Sheldon," said Mr. Harrison, "this is a wagon which will fill our every need. It is simply beautiful. The canvas is of such good material that no rain could ever penetrate it and ruin the contents."

"Also," said Mr. Sheldon, "look at its body with its high sides. It certainly looks like a boat, doesn't it?"

"It certainly does," answered Mr. Harrison. "There must be a reason for this."

"There is one. If you should come to a body of water which is so deep the horses can't wade across and the wagon would fill up with water, you can make it into a boat by detaching the wheels. The horses could swim across the body of water pulling the boat. After it and the horses reach the other side, the wheels can be reattached and you can be on your way. Some people call it a prairie schooner. I believe a schooner is a ship with two masts. So this one can travel across both prairies and water," explained Mr. Sheldon.

"This is nice to know, but I hope we never will come to a body of water on our way to Michigan which we can't ford across. The pigs are good swimmers, the horses are good swimmers, but I am afraid the sheep's wool would get water soaked and they would drown.

"If this ever happened, we could unload the wagons and carry the sheep across in them. After they are on the other side, we could return and bring back the wagon's contents," suggested Mr. Harrison.

"You are a good thinker and problem solver," commented Mr. Sheldon, "I believe you are able to tackle any problem which might arise on this Michigan trip."

"When will you deliver it, Mr. Sheldon?" asked Mr. Harrison.

"My delivery man will have it at your farm tomorrow at eleven o'clock," Mr. Sheldon replied.

"I will pay you right now whatever you ask," said Mr. Harrison.

As Mr. Harrison left the wagon store, he began to ask himself many questions. Was he imposing on his family in depriving his children the opportunity of receiving an education? He thought of the school they were attending, of their eagerness to learn, yes, and of the church in which they were active.

He not only thought of the deprivations he would be forcing on them, but of Martha, his dear, talented wife. She was a pillar in the church, a choir director, a Sunday School teacher. In fact, she was capable of filling any office where she was needed.

Mr. Harrison continued thinking, "If I remain in Ohio, I will lose everything, so we must leave."

CHAPTER 17 - AN EXCITING WELCOME

"Good boy, Brownie," said Mr. Harrison. "We have had a long trip today and it will be wonderful to be back home again, won't it?"

Brownie's feet sped over the country road. He knew they would soon be entering the driveway that connected the farm yard with the road. He did not know exactly what his rider meant, but he was such a smart horse that he had an idea that something nice was about to happen.

The older children were playing a game and did not know when the travelers arrived, but someone knew. She was only three and did not know how to play the game, so Almira stood waiting by a fence separating the back yard from the road. Suddenly she heard the sound of Brownie's galloping feet. "Daddy's here! Brownie's here!" she yelled as loudly as she could.

The older children jumped up and ran like a flash to the driveway. They began to smother their father with hugs and kisses. "Now, now," said Father Harrison. "I can't hug and kiss you all at once. Why don't you take turns?"

After the children had quieted down, their father saw Almira toddling toward him. But all of a sudden she lost her balance and down she went.

"Oh! my darling Allie," he said, "stay where you are and I will pick up up."

This tall handsome man who could be stern and firm yet kind, strode over to his youngest daughter and lifted her up in his big strong arms. "Oh! Daddy, Daddy, I am so glad you are home."

"I am happy to be home, too, Little Allie," he said.

Eight-year-old John, who was excited about the possibility of riding in a Conestoga, called to his father, "Daddy, did you find a Conestoga?"

"I certainly did," answered his father. "It will be delivered tomorrow and is it ever big and beautiful! It will take four horses to pull it. Some of the Conestogas are so large they require six horses to draw them. Then there are some which take only two. I am planning to have one of our smaller ones to be drawn by oxen. They are called covered wagons. Tomorrow the delivery man will deliver ours about eleven o'clock."

All of this time Brownie had quietly stood still waiting for his welcome attention. The children were so busy talking to their father they had forgotten him. But Brownie did not forget. He decided he would remind them. So, with a shake of his head and a "he, he, he" he let it be known that it was his turn to be loved.

Father Harrison spoke up, "Oh! Brownie, Brownie, if it had not been for you I could never have gone to Springfield." He went over to him and patted his lovely head. "You are a wonderful friend and we all love you, don't we children? They began to pat him, too. Allie wanted to have her turn, so Father Harrison put her right in the saddle so that she could pat his back.

Just then, Elias came from the barn. He exclaimed, "If it isn't Brownie and Dad who have come back to us. I think my horse must be hungry. Come on, pal, let's go to the barn for a rub down and a good supper of oats and a pail of cold water."

Brownie was very willing to follow Elias to the barn and did he ever enjoy his supper. He had traveled many miles that day and was very hungry. As soon as he finished eating he said, "He, he, he," and Elias said, "Good boy, Brownie."

In the next chapter you will learn why Mr. Harrison had the courage to take 116 animals and 21 people on such a perilous journey.

CHAPTER 18 - FATHER HARRISON
TAKES COMMAND

The next morning the family could hardly wait to see the big wagon. There was much excitement about its size and what it looked like.

The children were good workers and Father Harrison kept them busy digging carrots, potatoes and all the good vegetables which had grown so abundantly that summer.

At the breakfast table, he said to the family, "When the dogs begin to bark, you will know the Conestoga is here and I am giving you some rules which you must implicitly follow. Do you understand?"

"Yes, Father," said 13-year old Martha, "tell us what they are and we will do as you say." The children were accustomed to obeying their father and mother in every respect.

Father Harrison was unusually kind, but still he could be stern. Very seldom did he punish them, get angry or raise his voice. They had been brought up to never question any of his commands. Mother Harrison was also an excellent disciplinarian.

"Now this is my order," continued their father. "When you hear the dogs bark and the big wagon comes up the drive, stay where you are. If you should run to meet it, your noise might frighten the two horses that will be pulling it.I suppose they are accustomed to barking dogs, but probably they are not used to a running, yelling group of children. As soon as the horses are untied, Elias will take them to the enclosed spot behind the barn where they can graze awhile. Then, we will ask the delivery man to have dinner with us. After he has left and the dishes are washed and dried, please meet me on the back porch. You will then walk in an orderly fashion to examine the wagon."

You see, Father and Mother Harrison had special gifts in the organization of any activity. Their household ran like a clock and there was seldom any confusion.

As we continue on in our story, we will find Mr. Harrison was a great man with leadership ability. Because of these attributes, he had no qualms in undertaking such a monumental task as moving his family to an unknown territory.

The hours dragged by. It would soon be time for the arrival of the wagon at eleven o'clock. Everything was quiet, except for the children's conversation as they kept on digging those precious vegetables. The kind neighbors were planning to perserve them for the following winter. A wonderful aroma from Mother Harrison's kitchen drifted out on the breeze.

The dinner she was preparing smelled appetizingly delicious and the children were hungry.

At last, at eleven-thirty, the dogs began to bark as they always did when newcomers arrived.

Father Harrison and Elias were working in the cornfield gathering sweet corn which was going to be preserved for winter. When the two men heard the dogs, they ran to the drive to execute their plan.

In the next chapter, we will learn, along with the Harrison children, the characteristics of a Conestoga wagon and why the pioneers used them to "Go West."

CHAPTER 19 - ALMIRA AND HER PIGGY BACK RACE

After a good meal and the delivery man had left, everyone congregated on the back porch. "Dad," said eight-year old John, "why don't we have a race? Let's see who can be the first to reach the Conestoga."

"That is a good idea," said his father. "Do you want me to start you off?"

"Yes, do," said John. This was not the first time the children had run a race. They loved the competition and never argued over the judge's decision.

"After you arrive, stand in line and you may all have turns exploring the wagon. I will also try to answer your questions."

"Goody, goody," said Almira. She never could win a race, but she did not cry about it. She knew her legs were shorter than the others. Bazel Junior knew his little sister could never win this one, so he thought of a plan which would help him and Almira reach the goal a lot sooner.

"Here, Allie," he said, "jump up on my back and we will run piggy back style. Won't that be fun?"

"It sure will, do you really mean that you and I will be running the race together?"

"That's just what I mean. Now, when I stoop down you jump on my back," replied Bazel Junior. He loved his little sister so much that he liked to do things which would make her happy. He stooped down, "One, two, three, now jump," he said. And Allie did jump right on Bazel's back. They went over to where everyone was waiting in line.

"I guess we are all here," said Father Harrison. "Are your ready? All right, on your mark, get set, go." Off everyone ran as fast as possible. Bazel Junior was falling behind. "Oh! Allie," he said, "I am afraid we won't win." "Yes, we can," answered Allie, "just hurry a little faster."

Allie's encouraging words seemed to give him new strength. He began to run faster. Pretty soon he was catching up and to make a long story short, he and Allie did win the race, even though it was piggy back style. When everyone was praising him for his success, he said, "It was all because of Allie, give her the credit. She told me I could win if I just ran a little faster."

Little did Bazel Junior realize at age 14 that someday he would remember Allie's words when he became a medical student and the going was rough. He would recall her words, "You can win, yes, you can."

Did Bazel Junior win? Did he achieve his dream to become a doctor? A later chapter of this story will tell.

CHAPTER 20 - THE SHOW OFF

After the excitement of the race and everyone had finished congratulating Almira and Bazel Junior, Father Harrison called out, "It's time for us to look at the Conestoga." The children spread themselves in a semi-circle around one side of it.

Eight-year-old John began, "Dad," he said, "what a large, large wagon. I never realized it would be this big."

"I didn't either," commented 17-year-old Worlenda. "How many horses will it take to pull it?"

"I like your questions," answered Father Harrison. "This wagon requires four horses, but there are bigger wagons than this. The real large ones must have six or eight."

"But, Dad," continued John, "where does the driver sit? The front of the wagon seems to have no place for him. The cover seems to be pulled shut and it looks like the hole in front is used to let in the light."

"Well, John, this is another good question," replied his father. "Can you picture four horses together, two in front and two in back? You see the driver will sit on the rear horse, which is on the left side."

Now John had a good picture in his mind of just where the driver would sit. He walked to the place where the riding horse would be. He pretended he was the driver of an imaginary one.

He made believe he jumped on the horse, picked up the reins and said, "giddap." John loved to dramatize stories and he was a good actor.

"You are correct, John," said Father Harrison, "you have the right idea. You will not be driving one horse, but all four horses. You would have all four reins in your hands. I think our horses will quickly respond to the driver's commands. It is quite a trick to do this, but we men will have to practice this feat."

Questions began to rise in 13-year old Martha's mind. She noticed the large wheels. "Dad," she asked, "why are those wheels so much bigger than the wheels on our smaller wagons?"

"Martha," he said, "if the wheels were not large, the body of the wagon would be apt to strike the ruts in the uneven road. Or, in other words, the body must be high from the road. If it were not, the bottom of the wagon would soon be worn to pieces just from hitting those uneven places. Do you see this?"

"I certainly do," she answered.

John spoke up again. "Dad," he said, "the rims on the wheels seem so much wider than the rims on our wagons. Why is this?"

"You see, John," answered his father, "if the rims were small and the wheels were large, in addition to the wagon being heavy, the wheels might get stuck in mud puddles. Then it would be difficult for the horses to pull it out of the oozy mess."

Mother Harrison had finished her work in the kitchen and had just joined the family. She was becoming very interested in this huge wagon. "Look children," she said, as she touched the sides of the wagon. "To me the lower part looks just like a boat. See how the sides slope or slant upward or perhaps I should say outward. Now, Dad, I think I should ask a question."

"What do you want to know, Mother?" questioned her husband.

"I would like to know why a wagon should be built like a boat."

"Mother, you have hit on a good question," answered Bazel, Senior. "Do you know children, Mother is asking the same question I asked Mr. Sheldon, the salesman at the wagon store. I will tell you what he told me. Sometimes a Conestoga wagon is called a Prairie Schooner. There is a certain kind of ship called a schooner. A Conestoga may come to a river and, if the river is too deep for crossing or we call it fording, and the horses feet can't touch bottom, the wheels are removed and the horses swim across the water, pulling the waterproof floating wagon. As soon as it reaches the other side, the wheels are attached again. A pretty good invention, isn't it?"

"It certainly is," commented Worlenda. "I think my teacher told us about a prairie schooner."

"Do you have any other questions?" asked

their father. "I do," answered Almira, who was trying to learn her colors. "Our wagons don't have anything on top of them. This one has something white all over it."

"You see, honey," said her father, "we may have rain or snow while we are traveling. The cover is made of canvas and nothing can get wet underneath it. Your next questions will probably be why is the bottom painted blue."

"Yes, Dad," said Bazel Junior, "tell us why."

"Son," answered Father Harrison, "perhaps it is blue like the sky. We never tire watching the blue sky, do we? Perhaps whoever invented the Conestoga said to himself, I will paint the body blue, because this color is so easy on the eyes."

"Let's look inside," said Martha, "I can't wait to see it."

"Before we do, I must tell you to be careful. You may step up into the wagon from the rear. I have pulled the curtains aside. Here is a stool which will make it easier for you. But as you walk around, be extra careful. Since the sides slope or slant outward, it will be difficult for you to touch them to keep your balance," warned their father.

Bazel Junior said, "I will be last to do my exploring." He decided to show off. He would do something different. When it was his turn to explore the wagon, he began to hop on one foot. The next thing he knew he was on the floor. He had lost his balance and fell. As he did so he turned his ankle.

"Dad, oh, Dad," he called. "I'm sorry, I wasn't careful like you said I should be. I was hopping on one foot. It hurts, Dad, it pains. I can't stand it."

Elias, who had just arrived wanted to see the wagon. "Come here, Elias, help me," called Father Harrison. "You take one arm and I will take the other. We will take him outside, then you hitch Ned to the brown wagon and we will take him to Dr. Cooke."

Did Bazel Junior's fall turn out to be a good thing? Let us read the next chapter to find out.

CHAPTER 21 - BAZEL JUNIOR MEETS DR. COOKE

As the wagon came into the drive, Dr. Cooke was looking out of his window. He said to himself, "Well, well, if it isn't Mr. Harrison, Elias and Bazel Junior. I wonder what has happened that is bringing them to my office. I hope nothing terrible has taken place."

He watched the three as they walked up the drive to his office,which was located in his home. Bazel Junior held tightly to his father's and Elias' arms.

"Come in, come in," greeted Dr. Cooke in a pleasant voice. "Just what have you done to your ankle, Bazel Harrison the Second?"

"I don't know. I want you to tell me, Dr. Cooke. I know it pains and hurts. I hope you can do something about it," replied Bazel Junior in a whimpering voice.

"Why don't all of you step into my inner office and take some chairs. There are two just waiting for you, Mr. Harrison, and for your son Elias. Now, young man, I will help you jump up on my examining table. Here, take my arm and I will give you a boost."

After Bazel Junior was comfortably seated on the table, Dr. Cooke said, "You should not walk on your foot for several days. Your ankle is very swollen and I want you to soak it in cool water four times a day for about half an hour each time. You may hop on the good foot, but be careful and don't step on the other one. Luckily, you do not have a break or sprain. You just twisted it, which should quickly heal. I want to see you again in three days."

After Mr. Harrison paid the bill and had made an appointment for the next visit, the two men helped Bazel Junior hop to the wagon. Brownie was patiently waiting. Elias didn't tie him as he knew his beloved horse would never walk away.

As they passed him on the way to the wagon, Elias gave him a loving pat saying, "Good boy, Brownie." He in turn returned this show of affection with a shake of his head and a little whinny, "He, he, he."

After a few miles, the trotting Brownie turned into the Harrison drive with his precious family. He knew this was where he lived and Father Harrison, who was driving, did not have to remind him that this was home.

CHAPTER 22 - HOPPITY HOP HOP RETURNS TO DR. COOKE

The next three days after Bazel Junior's trip to see Dr. Cooke, all he could do to move around was to hop. His family called him "Hoppity Hop Hop."

He said to himself, "I wanted to act smart, I was nothing but a show off. Dad told us to be careful when we walked around in our new Conestoga. The sloping sides would be of no help in my keeping my balance. But I paid no attention to him. I began to hop around in it and my fall was the result. Now all I can do is hop. This is hard work. It is much easier to just sit and I don't like to sit. No, I don't! Dad always knows best. This experience has taught me a lesson. From now on I will obey him. I know Dad wants us to start for Michigan as soon as possible and I trust my foolishness will not delay his plans."

After the three days had passed, Elias came to Bazel Junior. "You know, brother," he said, "this is the day we must return to see Dr. Cooke. I hope you will soon be walking normally again because you will be needed to guide the animals on our trip to Michigan. Perhaps Dad has not told you, but he is planning to take fifty sheep and fifty hogs. Of course, they will have to walk since we do not have enough wagons to carry all of them. You, John, and the dogs will have the responsibility of keeping them from straying away from the group."

Since Bazel Junior's ankle appered to be quite normal, Elias said to his young brother, "Why don't we ride Brownie instead of taking the wagon?"

"That suits me, Elias, I don't think I will have any trouble mounting him."

Soon the two brothers were bouncing up and down, synchronizing with the rhythm of Brownie's galloping. It was a warm day in August. The soft breeze blew against their faces. The green grass in the pastures, in addition to the gorgeous hues of flowers along the roadside, formed a beautiful picture.

Before the time of Bazel Junior's appointment, Dr. Cooke was in his office doing some thinking. If he could have expressed his thoughts audibly they might have taken the following course, "I can't believe what neighbor Bush told me this morning. He said that Bazel Harrison must be out of his mind. Why, he is taking 50 sheep and 50 hogs to Michigan. Doesn't he know that hogs, at the first sight of a mud puddle, will scatter and the next thing they will all be wallowing around in the oozy goo? Doesn't he know that sheep will have all kinds of problems? They aren't built to walk a long distance. Some of the sheep might leave the group and start eating the green grass along the side of the woods. He is a very foolish man."

After Mr. Bush had left, another patient came for his appointment, a close neighbor of the Harrisons. As he came into the office, Dr. Cooke began to tell him about Mr. Bush's comments regarding this foolish venture. "I am very glad you came, Mr. Johnson. I am worried about Bazel Harrison's trip to Michigan. It will be very dangerous to enter an unknown territory, especially when he is taking all those animals. You live close to him and perhaps you can influence him to at least sell the animals."

Did Mr. Johnson go along with Dr. Cooke's idea to influence Mr. Harrison to eliminate the animals on the trip? The next chapter will answer this question.

CHAPTER 23 - MR. JOHNSON SPEAKS UP

"Well, well," answered Mr. Johnson. "You don't know Mr. Harrison like I do. My farm borders his and I am not worried one bit about his being out of his mind. You see, for several years I have been observing him and I've come to the conclusion that he knows what he is doing.

"If you could see him handle those sheep and swine you would think that he is an animal trainer. They adore him and will obey his every command. John and Bazel Jr. are also capable and have been trained by their father to efficiently care for them. As far as walking all the way to Michigan, I have seen Mr. Harrison, the boys and the dogs practicing on the road. You probably realize that pigs are fast runners, so they have no trouble in walking fast and it is interesting to see those sheep trying to keep up. I think encouragement is half the battle and it is amazing how animals behave and hurry along with the praise and affection that are showered on them. Mr. Harrison told me, too, that he will have his cavalcade walk short distances each day so the animals will not become too tired.

"Another asset that will help him with his decisions is his excellent mind. Mr. Harrison told me about one of ancestors, the great General William Harrison, who received a commission from the famous English government official Oliver Cromwell. He isn't bragging, but I believe he is just proud to be related to him. You and I know that intelligence is inherited. So, I believe our neighbor, no doubt, has many of his abilities. It will take real ability to do what he is about to do."

"Thank you, Mr. Johnson," said Dr. Cooke, "for the things you have told me. I am beginning to have faith in our neighbor, that he is very capable and will accomplish whatever he has sets out to do."

"I must leave now, but I am glad to know you are changing your mind about Mr. Harrison," responded Mr. Johnson.

In a later chapter you will find out who Mr. Harrison's famous ancestors were and if he, too, became a great man.

CHAPTER 24 - DR. COOKE'S IDEA

After Mr. Johnson had left, Dr. Cooke remembered some other words he had said. They went something like this, "You know, Dr. Cooke, I have heard that your patient Bazel Harrison the Second seems to have an ability for making sick animals well. I believe he can go to his mother's cupboard and find ingredients, that, if mixed in the right proportions, have healing powers. The family is also interested in growing herbs and you and I know that there are certain ones that can be effective in relieving pain. I believe this young man has been interested in experimenting with them, also. I just wonder if he should be encouraged to go to medical school."

Just as Dr. Cooke was pondering over these thoughts, Elias and Bazel Junior arrived. He was pleased with Bazel Junior's progress. "I think you have done well in taking care of the ankle, young man, and you should be able to take over your position of guiding the animals as they travel to Michigan. Your neighbor, Mr. Johnson, has told me about your ability to handle your sheep and swine. I know your family and neighbors will be able to complete this journey with wonderful success.

"I have heard, Bazel Junior, that you lean toward the field of medicine. I encourage you, when you are old enough, to consider entering medical school. In order to inspire you, I am giving you several of my medical books which may come in handy, especially as you are traveling. Would you like them?"

"Oh! would I?" answered Bazel Junior.

"You see, a country doctor must be able to take care of sick animals as well as sick people," Dr. Cooke continued. "Perhaps on your trip a cow might have something wrong with her. If you know the symptoms, you could look up the malady in this book and it will explain what you can do to relieve the pain. Usually you can make concoctions out of ingredients your mother may have for cooking.

"The other book tells about diseases of people. Take them with you. Read them and when you are old enough to become a doctor, there may be a medical school in your community."

"Oh, thank you, Dr. Cooke," replied Bazel Junior, "You don't know how much you have encouraged me."

Just then, Elias appeared. "We must be leaving, but this has been nice to really know you, Dr. Cooke, and we will never forget you, even when we are in Michigan."

"Good-bye to both of you and please tell your father I think he is a great man and that he will be greater still in starting a new community up there in Michigan."

Did this band of pioneers arrive safely at their destination and did Mr. Harrison become a great leader in the new community?

CHAPTER 25 - THE INVITATION

Several days after Mr. Harrison had made his decision to travel to Michigan, he said to his wife, "Martha, I believe we should invite some of our relatives and neighbors to go with us. What do you think?"

"I certainly feel this is an excellent idea. Elias has said that we may have to cut down trees in order to make a way for the wagons to go through the wooded areas. I guess we will be the first people to ever travel this route by way of a wagon train. He also said there are wolves that will howl at night, but I understand they do not like fire and as long as we keep one burning, they will stay in their places. "

Just then Elias appeared. He joined the conversation saying, "Yes, Dad, this means we will need several men to make the trip. You and I could never chop down enough trees to clear a path. Neither would we be able to gather enough wood to keep the fires burning all night, let alone tending it. If it dies down those wolves would pounce on us and quicker than scat they would be having a feast on pork roast, people roast and lamb chops. They sure enjoy the flavor of the latter, I am told. It just makes sense to me. The more men we have, the easier our trip will be."

"Martha and Elias, " replied Father Harrison, "you are correct and today I shall try to recruit volunteers to go with us."

The first person Mr. Harrison asked to go was his oldest son William. "Yes, Dad, I would like to join your party, but I can't leave my business right now. I will probably come next year."

When Ephraim, another one of the Harrison sons was invited, he answered "Yes, Dad, I have no ties here and I can take my blacksmith position with me. No doubt, after we arrive, more families will arrive from the East. They will bring their horses and there will be a need for a blacksmith to make shoes for their horses. I am sure my wife will be anxious to go, so with the children, there will be five of us."

The next person Father Harrison asked to join them was his son-in-law Henry Whipple and his wife, the former Cynthia Harrison. "Oh! Dad," he said, "I welcome the chance to accompany you and I know Cynthia would want to go wherever her father and mother go. I am glad we are just renting our farm, so there will be no real estate problems." With their two children, this made a total of 11 people.

Two neighbors, Abraham Davidson and his brother Ephraim, volunteered to go. With his wife and child the number of brave souls rose to 15. So, counting the unmarried Harrison children, the final number came to 21 people. Included in this family were Elias, 24; Worlenda, 17; Bazel Jr., 14; Martha, 13; John, 8; and Almira, 3.

CHAPTER 26 - THE BUZZING BEES

When the word spread that the Harrison family was leaving the well populated state of Ohio to travel to the unknown territory of Michigan, their neighbors became very excited. You see, they were in the habit of sharing their talents. They believed the old adage, "A friend in need is a friend indeed." As problems arose in this friendly community, the people joined together lending helping hands to needy neighbors.

Now they realized if ever there were friends who could use their help, it was the Bazel Harrison family. They called a meeting and they organized groups. They knew they must work fast in order to help their friendly neighbors prepare for the coming adventure.

The summer had been an excellent one for growing crops. The sun shone and the right amount of rain fell, producing an abundant harvest. Mr. Harrison said to his wife, "This is a miracle. If ever we needed a good crop, it is now." "Yes, Bazel," she said, "We're in the hands of the One who gave us all the sun and rain. We are indeed grateful."

When the neighbors announced their intentions to harvest the grain, to pick the fruit, to smoke, to pickle, to do the necessary salting and drying of food, Father Harrison said, "Our buzzing bee friends are instigators of another miracle."

Mr. Carpenter, who appeared to be the leader of the Buzzing Bee Club, came to Mr. Harrison. He explained, "We will see that your wagons are packed with barrels of food for both those who are going with you and also for the animals. With your hunting and fishing to supplement, you should have enough food to last all winter and into the spring. I hear you are taking 50 sheep and 50 swine. You shouldn't lack for meat. Three cows will certainly supply you with all the milk you need. If you can find room for some crates, it wouldn't hurt to take some hens and roosters."

"Thank you, Mr. Carpenter," replied Mr. Harrison. "I certainly appreciate all you are doing. I am so happy I can't keep back my tears."

Just then, Mr. Jones, another neighbor, appeared. "You certainly deserve any help we can give you. We have watched you dear neighbors and we believe you are a great leader. When you arrive in Michigan as more and more people come, you will continue to be great. I would not be surprised to hear that your name will be one to go down in history. We will need your help in telling us where to put everything in the wagons in an orderly fashion. We are planning to organize all items in such a way that when you need anything in particular, you will be able to find it."

In a future chapter, you will find out if Mr. Jones predictions really did come true.

CHAPTER 27 - THE BIG DAY

September 19, 1828, the day before the departure of the wagon train arrived. The neighbors had planned a farewell potluck supper to be held at the Sellers' farm. The final night arrived. Farmers and their families were crowded around the tables which had been set up on the beautiful lawn of this well-to-do family. Mr. Harrison was so well-known and respected that people had come from miles around to bid the family good-bye. As more guests arrived carrying their picnic baskets to the tables, the aroma of outdoor cooking combined with the many dishes of food, whetted their appetites.

When all the food had been placed on the table and everyone was ready to eat, Mr. Sellers took a hammer and pounded one of the tables. Everyone stopped talking. All eyes turned on the host. Mr. Harrison was standing beside him. "Friends of this community," he began, "we have gathered together tonight to pay our respect to the one standing beside me, his family and all of those going with him. We know how they are starting out tomorrow to face the unknown, but the One who guided them through the years will continue to do so. I am asking Mr. Harrison to ask the blessing on this food. After we are finished eating, we will remain seated for a meeting to express our farewell wishes."

Mr. Harrison, who was in the habit of having morning and evening devotions, was equal to the occasion. His voice rang out loud and clear as he thanked his Heavenly Guide for the miracles and blessings he and his family had enjoyed. His words were few as he knew everyone was hungry. He would have another chance in the evening meeting to really express his gratefulness in an uninhibited way.

After everyone had finished eating, these beloved neighbors had a short time of expressing how much the Harrison family meant to each one and how their lives had been influenced by this great man and his family.

Both Mr. and Mrs. Harrison were asked to give farewell talks. As the meeting came to a close, tears were shed, but there were also expressions of faith, joy and hope.

These kind neighbors had invited each member of the wagon train to stay with them for the night and to share breakfast the next morning. With beds, blankets, food and dishes all packed, the travelers were indeed grateful for this invitation.

After a good night's rest, our future settlers arose to a warm sunny day, a day that would not hold them back in any way, shape or manner. Every one gathered at the Harrison farm where the wagon train was organized for the trip. As they arrived they saw the white covered wagons had been placed in order, with the gleaming and beautiful blue Conestoga in the lead.

The horses were hitched to their wagons;

the oxen were yoked to theirs and the three cows were tethered to the rear of one. Since the sheep would be somewhat slower than the other animals, they would lead the procession and set the pace. However, later they would be mixed in order for the pigs to stimulate the sheep to walk faster.

Bazel Junior, John and the dogs had come to their old farm earlier and had escorted the sheep and swine out to the road. The ladies were to drive the wagons while Elias and the men rode the horses. One man would drive all four of the horses hitched to the Conestoga. If walking became too much for John and Bazel Junior, two of the men would take their places while the boys rested.

This morning some of the neighbors came to say their last good-byes and to walk with the wagon train as far as they could. The sounds coming from the animals must have been almost deafening at times, "Oink, oink, baa, baa, he, he, he, moo, moo" blended with the barking of the dogs.

There was very little confusion as Mr. Harrison had everything under control. Finally the starting signal was given. The sheep and swine moved forward under the command of Bazel Junior and John. The drivers of the wagons gave their order of "giddap, giddap". One could hear the scraping of the wagon wheels as they started forward.

The neighbors, with tears in their eyes,

walked as far as they possibly could before they said their final good-byes and returned to their homes.

The families were off to a good start, realizing that they were leaving their homes for good and not knowing what was before them. But they were stalwart, brave and courageous and would keep the faith their forefathers had when they came to America.

An authentic covered wagon, which is on display at the Museum of Science and Industry in Chicago, is much like the four wagons the Harrisons used when they traveled to Michigan.

CHAPTER 28 - THE TRAIN SETS OUT OR ON THEIR WAY

At this time Mr. Harrison was hale and hearty, a man of 57 years. His health was excellent and he was just the person needed to be in command of this adventurous group.

The first town in their path was a busy little place named Urbana. From here they traveled west to Piqua and north along the banks of the Miami River to Sidney. They left the river and went onto St. Mary's. They crossed the state line into Indiana. There were no more corn fields. But as they came into Fort Wayne, the corn was again abundant.

As our 21 people left this city, they left civilization. From now on the only people they would see would be Indians. They were friendly and wondered about this procession of wagons and noisy animals. They wanted to be friends and showed this with smiles and gestures.

This would be the day the travelers would start the dangerous part of the journey. They had been following roads that were wide enough for the wagons to travel. Everything had gone along smoothly, but today would be different!

Just as the road ended and became an Indian trail, each of the 21 travelers knew they would have to depend on faith and faith alone to see them through.

Bazel Harrison realized the unknown lay ahead. Just before they were to take this step, the day of traveling had come to a close. They had reached a stream of water and a good camping place.

Since the animals were limited as to the number of miles they were able to travel, Mr. Harrison commanded that his party stop early in the afternoon to make camp. This would make it possible for them to graze and rest. Much wood would be needed to keep the fire burning all night. The ladies would have to prepare the one big meal for the day. Wild game was plentiful and some of the men would hunt for rabbits, wild turkeys and deer.

Three green sticks which could withstand the heat were put together making a tripod for hanging a kettle. This way, by adding vegetables and potatoes to the meat, a delicious stew could be prepared. Johnny cake was baked in a covered pan placed in a bed of hot ashes.

If the sun was warm, clothes were washed and hung over low branches or bushes to dry.

In the evening, Mr. Harrison conducted a devotional service that included Bible reading, prayer and the singing of old songs of the faith such as "Come Thou Almighty King" and "O God, Our Help in Ages Past." After this quiet pause, everyone retired for the night, except for those taking turns keeping the fire burning. The fire tenders had to be on the alert for wolves or any other dangers lurking near the camp. Another responsibility was to keep the animals from straying away. In the next chapter, we will have a story about the problems our pioneer friends confronted.

Mrs. Harrison said to Almira, "This is the lantern used when I looked for our cow, Lula Belle, the night she was ill. I must change the worn down candle for a new one."

CHAPTER 29 - BAZEL JUNIOR COMES TO THE RESCUE

It had been a peaceful evening. The cows had been milked and the sheep were examined for bruises and insect bites. Oil had been applied to sooth sores. The horses and oxen were sleeping and the pigs were quiet. The younger children were sleeping in the wagons, covered with snugly blankets their mothers had made from the sheep's wool.

Almira had been sleeping for quite some time. Worlenda, Martha and Mother Harrison were getting ready to spend the night in their covered wagon. The men who were not doing guard duty were sleeping on blankets on the ground.

Everything was pretty quiet, except for the screams of the wild animals that came from the surrounding area. Our discoverers became accustomed to these sounds and tried not to let them spoil their sleep.

Suddenly, as Worlenda was putting on her long nightdress and night cap, she thought she heard a sound that was new to her. "Mother," she said, "do you hear that? It sounds as if a baby is crying."

"Why, I believe I do hear it, said Mother Harrison. "you girls stay here with Almira and I will investigate. Martha, please bring me the lantern. I think I will need it."

Mother Harrison picked up the lantern

and started toward the source of the crying. Soon she heard it again, "Moooo, moooo, moooo."

"Why, it sounds as if one of the cows is in pain," she thought. She followed the sound, being careful not to step on the sleeping cows. Soon she discovered that it came from Lula Belle. "Oh! Lula Belle, it is you crying!" When the cow heard Mother Harrison's voice, her crying became louder.

"Now, now, you are a very sick cow. I don't know what to do for you. We have a blacksmith with us, but he can't help you. How I wish we had a veterinarian in the camp."

Then Mrs. Harrison had a pleasant thought. "Why we do, we do have a future veterinarian. It is my son Bazel Junior. I believe he was studying the medical books Dr. Cooke gave him by the fire tonight. I know what I will do. I will ask him to look at the book on treating sick animals. I will find him and just hope he can figure out what is wrong with Lula Belle."

"Oh, Bazel dear," said Mother Harrison. "I believe Lula Belle is very ill. Will you please come and look at her. Perhaps you can find something about her ailment in Dr. Cooke's book on animal diseases."

"I will come right now. I have been studying that particular book this evening. You see, back home Dad used to ask me to help him when anything went wrong with the animals. Usually, if we gave them the right treatment,

Usually, if we gave them the right treatment, they revived. Dad used to say I should be a doctor."

Mother Harrison went to the wagon and told Bazel Junior to take her lantern until he could find another one.

He examined Lula Belle, then returned to his veterinarian book and found that her trouble was described with the necessary treatment. The solution the book prescribed could easily be made with herbs and other ingredients his mother had stored in a cupboard in the Conestoga. He found that Lula Belle had punctured the skin of one of her legs and it left an ugly red would. He realized something must be done right away to relieve her pain. He followed the treatment recommended in the book called *Animal Diseases*, by Doctor E. P. Wooden. After he finished applying the solution he had made by mixing the suggested ingredients, Lula Belle quieted down and was soon fast asleep.

The next day was Sunday, which Mr. Harrison observed as a day of rest. He also encouraged the members of the wagon camp to do so as well. This gave a day for Lula Belle to rest and be off of her leg. The following morning as everyone was enjoying a leisurely breakfast around the camp fire, the topic of discussion was the events of Saturday evening.

Just as there was much rejoicing after the night of the confrontation with the wolves, which you will hear about in another chapter, so this morning you can imagine the joy that prevailed. Bazel Junior was nicknamed "Doctor B" and was given much respect for the knowledge he displayed in saving the life of Lula Belle.

A cow like Lula Belle from an 1859 book.

CHAPTER 30 - RUNTY GRUNTY

In order to understand the story of Puddlin' Pigs in Chapter 31, in which Almira plays an important role, let us look back several months to the spring of 1828, a season when baby animals are born.

This story took place before the Harrisons decided to move West. Spring had come and this is the time of year when baby animals are born.

It was May 9th, 1828, and Mr. Harrison knew that Porky Pig would soon have baby pigs. However, he did not know just when these little piggies were to be born. As he walked in the barn this beautiful warm day, he heard some strange sounds. "I wonder, I wonder," he said to himself, "if Porky Pig has had her babies." He walked to the corner of the barn where she usually slept. There he saw her lying down and what do you think he saw and heard? There were ten little piglets, all trying to suck Mother Pig's nipples. They were hungry and they wanted their breakfast of milk.

But those ten little piglets were having a great problem. Mother Pig had only nine nipples. Did you ever have a bottle with a nipple? Then you know what a nipple is. The difference is your nipple was attached to a bottle and Mother Pig had her nipples spread out under her body. Remember, now, there were ten piglets and there were only nine nipples. If this were the

the case, one piggy would have to go without milk.

Father Harrison looked at all ten piglets. He noticed there was one little piggy that was smaller than the others. He was trying to push a bigger piggy out of the way so he could drink, too, but all the rest of the piglets were bigger, so they gave him a great big shove.

"Oh, you little runt," said Father Harrison, "you are just too small to push your brother or sister aside so you can drink also. Something must be done about this." Then he had a thought. "I will pick up the little runt and take him to Almira. Maybe she will feed him."

Father Harrison tenderly picked him up and carried him in his arms to the kitchen. Almira was just finishing her breakfast.

"Allie, Allie," he he said, "would you like a baby piggy for a pet? You could hold him in your arms, cuddle him and love him. You will have to learn how to feed him, but I think I can invent some kind of bottle so you won't have any problem. You see, dear, his mother has too many piglets and she cannot feed all of them."

"Daddy, daddy," said Almira, "do you mean this piggy will really be mine?"

"Yes, he will be all yours. He will love you because you are good to him and will be giving him his milk."

So Almira became the "mother" of Runty Grunty and did he ever love her! Did she return his love? Oh! yes she did. She played with him, she held him in her arms until he grew so big she could not lift him. But they went for walks together and he was her pet.

In the next story you will hear about Runty Grunty again. You see pigs are affectionate and smart. They can become real pets.

"Oh! Runty Grunty, you have been my pet for a long time now and I shall continue to keep you from ending on our dinner plate," eleven-year old Almira assures her pet.

CHAPTER 31 - THE PUDDLIN' PIGS

If you were to watch the pigs and the sheep leading the procession, you would probably be saying to yourself, "Now, Mr. Harrison, how do you expect to keep those swine from leaving the group and running away?

"Oh! those mud puddles made by recent rains, won't they be so enticing that your pigs just can't resist the temptation?

"What about your sheep? It will be hard for them to stay in line when they see the luscious green grass along the side of the road or path. They surely will be out there gazing away.

"The pigs can really run and they will try to walk faster than the sheep who will be poking along. Mark my word, you are going to have one problem after another keeping all of those animals together. You should never have brought them in the first place.

"However, if I am talking this way, I had better change my tune, When I really did see Mr. Harrison in action, I found him to be in full control."

He had trained eight-year-old John and 14-year-old Bazel Junior to walk beside the sheep and pigs, one boy on each side. Their helpers were none other than four sheep dogs, two on each side. With the help of a stick each boy was carrying and the intelligence of the trained dogs, the pigs and sheep walked along together. If one animal started to leave the line, the barking dogs brought it back.

Everything went along quite smoothly until one day and that day could have been a disaster if Mr. Harrison had not made a quick decision. You see, he is proving to be a real commander; not of an army, but of 50 sheep, 50 pigs, 11 horses, two oxen, three cows and 20 people.

Now you remember Almira was riding with her mother in a wagon that was just behind the Conestoga. Today, Mr. Harrison was driving the four horses that were pulling the wagon.

Almira had been given the responsibility of watching the side of the road and if she saw any pigs leave the line before her brothers or the dogs did, to report it to her mother.

Suddenly, as she was carefully watching from the wagon, she spied Runty Grunty. There he was running toward a mud puddle. When the other pigs saw what was happening, they started to follow him.

"Ma Ma," called Almira, "the pigs are running to the mud puddles." Mrs. Harrison called out loud and clear, "John, Bazel, watch the pigs.

Immediately, the word spread throughout the procession. Mr. Harrison realized what was happening. He saw a stream nearby. The travelers had been on the road several hours. so, he called out, "Everyone stop. Let's make camp. Let the pigs wallow in the mud puddles let the sheep start grazing." The horses were unhitched and allowed to graze, too.

Mr. Harrison could see there would be trouble if the boys tried to bring the pigs back in line. They were now having a wonderful time rolling in the deep mud. They all wanted to wallow in the same puddle, but when Mr. Harrison saw what was going on he urged them to spread out. Because of the recent rains, there were several puddles nearby.

Did those pigs ever have a good time! They squealed, they grunted, they rolled this way and they rolled that way. Finally, they just lay down in the mud and went to sleep.

Of course, when Runty Grunty had enough of the fun, he enjoyed having Almira near him. She talked to him and gave him lots of loving pats. The children had a wonderful time wading in the creek.

Some of the men began to chop wood for the fire. Some of them went hunting to see if they could shoot a goose, duck, rabbit or wild turkey to provide the campers with meat. Some of the ladies began to prepare food and cook it over the open fire.

Did the travelers meet other hardships? Let's read the next chapter to find out. After all, was the last story a hardship? I think the people and animals thought it to be a holiday. What do you think?

CHAPTER 32 - LEAVING CIVILIZATION

As mentioned earlier, after leaving Fort Wayne, the traveling would be anything but easy. There would no longer be well traveled roads, but only narrow paths which had been made by Indians and traders. Only trees,which were many, loomed in the way. This meant a delay as our hardy adventurers dug out their axes in order to cut trees down. The road which they had to make must be wide enough for the Conestoga to pass through. To save time, the sheep and pigs also needed a wide space which would accommodate their walking.

One day the wagon train was confronted with a swamp. Elias came to his father and said, "I guess we are in for a multitude of problems. It will take days to go around this swamp at the rate we are traveling. Brownie and I ran into this very same one on our trip to Michigan. However, we had no problem since we could go so much faster without the animals and wagons. But Dad, take heart. There is really an end to it."

The next day all they could see was water and weeds. It became quite monotonous to see that same scene day after day. Actually, they traveled seven days before it ended. When this experience was over, there was much shouting and rejoicing.

Another time, they came to a stream they

had to cross, but the water was so high our party had to travel several hours before finding a place shallow enough for them to cross.

They traveled so slowly that one evening as our friends looked backward, they could see the smoke still rising from the campfire they had left in the morning.

Every night they would hear the screams of the wild animals, but as long as there was a blazing fire, the critters would stay away. The members of this adventurous group had to learn this lesson the hard way.

In the next story you will read about an exciting night when the fire almost went out. If it had not been for Brownie, the camp might have been devastated and there would have been no one left to tell the story.

CHAPTER 33 - WOLVES ON THE PROWL

It had been about ten days since our brave families had left civilization.

The day had been long and tiring. Many trees had to be chopped down in order for the wagon train to have a large enough clearing to go through.

When it was time to retire, no one volunteered to keep the fire replenished with wood through the night.

Mr. Harrison realized the survival of all depended on the roaring fire that must not be allowed to die down.

After a devotional service when everyone was gathered around the fire, Mr. Harrison said, "I know you are all very tired, but we need someone who will stay awake for half of the night to keep the fire blazing. I will take either half."

No one said anything. Finally, Elias said, "Dad, these wolves' howls seem closer than they have been before. I am worried, so I will take the first watch. Brownie and I had an easier day than the rest of you. We went on a scouting trip to check out possible dangers which might lie ahead of us. Riding isn't nearly as hard as chopping down trees, so I guess I am fresh enough to do the job."

"Thank you, Elias," said his father. Bazel Junior spoke up, "Dad, I will help Elias by watching the animals. I don't want to see any wolf dragging one away. If I do see this, I will whistle to Elias."

"Thank you, son," replied Mr. Harrison. "By the way, I warn all of you men to have your flint lock rifles handy. I have a feeling that tonight we may have to let them know who is boss in this camp."

Everyone went to bed except the watchmen. If one can call sleeping on the hard ground or in the wagons "bed." The campers were so tired they were soon fast asleep.

Suddenly, the howls seemed to die down. All was very quiet. In fact, everything was so quiet the watchmen dozed off just long enough for the blazing fire to change to burning coals.

Not everyone was sleeping though. There was someone who sensed danger was near and felt he should stay awake. Who was that someone? It was none other than Brownie, whose sense of hearing was very keen. He could detect wild animals quite a distance away. Suddenly, he heard the brush crackling. He knew danger was coming closer! Something must be done. He could not let anything happen to his beloved master. "He, he, he, he," he whinnied and ran to the sleeping men. He put his head near Elias and continued his warning.

Suddenly Elias awakened and realized what had happened to the fire. There were some extra dry sticks nearby which he threw on the coals. At once, they burst into flames. By this time all of the men were awake. They added more dry wood and the fire began to roar.

Soon all of the men realized something had to be done. They grabbed their rifles and fired into the darkness. "Zing, zing," went the bullets. Then several yelps came from the thicket.

Mr. Harrison, who was awake now said, "I guess these fellows won't bother us the rest of the night."

Evidently, the wolves had come together as a pack and planned to sneak up on the sleeping people. This must have been the reason everything was quiet before the planned attack.

Of course, Brownie was given his fair share of praise and the men vowed they would never sleep again when they were on guard.

The following morning, as our courageous ones were having breakfast around the fire, everyone was rejoicing. Mr. Harrison gave a little talk on their guardian angels who had protected them from this terrible peril.

CHAPTER 34 - IS THIS THE PROMISED LAND?

Yes, the hardships were many, but these determined explorers had many compensations for their setbacks.

The woods were beautiful with the leaves having turned into gorgeous hues of red, green, gold and rust colors. Autumn seemed to be the best time to travel. The air was cool and crisp.

They found water to be plentiful in the streams due to the early fall rains. Each time they left a source of water, they filled barrels with the precious supply, in case they had to travel for some time without any. The large barrels were attached to the sides of the covered wagons.

The sheep were well taken care of as they would rise at the break of dawn and graze on any precious grass they could find. In doing so, they would drink the dew before the sun dried it up.

As our wagon train rolled along, the travelers would excitedly exclaim to one another, "Oh! see the tree at the right of us. I never saw anything like it in Ohio. It must be new."

When the train came to a lake, it looked like a silver looking glass. The trees surrounding it were one mass of gold. Our travelers were so delighted they were beginning to forget the hardships of the past few weeks. Elias said, "Take courage, dear ones. We are nearing the end of our journey."

The woods were full of various kinds of wild fruits. There was no want for meat, as game was abundant. The songs of birds floated over the air making our friends wonder if they had reached heaven.

They continued their trip across the plains of Goshen and over the beautiful Elkhart Prairie to the border line of Michigan. This beautiful land was very attractive. In fact, it was so enticing, some members of the party thought this should be the end of their journey. Henry Whipple, Mr. Harrison's son-in-law, made it known that he believed they should stop right here and settle in Indiana.

When Mr. Harrison heard how his relatives and neighbors felt, he called a meeting. "Friends and relatives," he said, "I know how you feel about the fact we have reached the Promised Land and this is where we should settle, but I think we should continue on. I believe there is a land farther north waiting for us. I realize this is a beautiful location, but you know we are still in Indiana. Indiana has been a state for 12 years.

"Let's enter Michigan. I think this territory is thinly populated and no doubt we will have the pick of the land. Traders have told me there are no homes, no white people and only friendly Indians. Of course, there are white traders and hunters, but they come and go."

Again, some of our travelers did not agree

with Mr. Harrison, especially Mr. Whipple, who, after some consideration of the matter said to his wife, Mr. Harrison's daughter, Cynthia, "I believe Dad is right. I feel now we should stick with him and the rest of the group. There is no one like your father. He has brought us through many hard places and remains cheerful and optimistic in spite of disturbing circumstances."

"Yes, Henry," said Cynthia, "I think my father is the greatest. There is no other who could take his place. We children highly respect him and his decisions. There is no reason for us to break our relationship and leave the rest of the group."

After this problem was resolved in such a diplomatic way, the wagon train continued to travel across the Elkhart Prairie.

CHAPTER 35 - SPYING OUT THE LAND

The day had gone quite smoothly with no problems confronting our pioneers. When three o'clock rolled around, Mr. Harrison sent word for everyone to stop and make camp at this very beautiful site which was located on Baldwin's Prairie.

As soon as the horses were unhitched and all the animals were grazing on tender green grass, Mr. Harrison called a meeting. He began, "Dear ones, I believe we are nearing our destination. I propose we send scouts to spy out the country north of here. We will consider this camp as a temporary one.

"I suggest Abraham Davidson, Henry Whipple, Elias and I saddle our horses and ride to this location. I do not know how long we will be gone, but I am sure Ephraim Davidson and my Ephraim will take good care of you who remain. If you should be accosted by any wild animals their flint lock rifles will solve the problem.

"We will take enough food to last a few days. However, to make this food last, we will have to 'eat off the land', as they say. We can fish and hunt muskrats, rabbits and other game. We will miss our good cooks and their food, but we will appreciate them more when we return. We will leave tomorrow morning."

The next day dawned bright and clear. Brownie sensed something different was happening. He knew preparations were being made for his friends to leave the camp. He was afraid he might be left behind. But, when Elias came to him and said, "Do you want to be my partner, Brownie? I can't go without you. You know we are going north and we may meet the same Indians who became our friends a year ago. Wouldn't that be wonderful?"

"He, he, he," whinnied Brownie.

Ephraim, the blacksmith, had checked the horses' shoes to see if they needed any repairing. He had brought the tools he used in his work. One horse was taken which would be riderless and carry the needed equipment.

After breakfast, Mr. Harrison committed each one of the scouts and those remaining behind to the care of their Heavenly Father.

As the group traveled north, they met several traders. These men asked the scouts where they were going.

"We hear there is some beautiful country just north of here which has never been settled," answered Elias. "I visited some Indians who lived very close to the border a year ago last summer. Have you seen this land?"

"We certainly have," answered one of the traders. "I believe you will find a great prairie, the largest in the territory. The soil is black and fertile and has never been farmed. You can't make a mistake if you bring your families up there to settle."

"Thank you," said Elias, "we appreciate

your advice."

The group of four men and five horses traveled on. After they had gone a short distance, they met four Indians. Perhaps you will remember that Elias learned enough Indian words to make them understand what they were seeking. The Indians confirmed every word of the traders.

Mr. Harrison said to his men, "Let us keep going north to see for ourselves if this wonderful report is true."

They traveled about 40 miles and to their amazement they came to a large, beautiful prairie covered with tall green spike grass. Dotting the landscape were flowers of gorgeous hues which had not been killed by the fall frosts.

As the wind came sweeping over this mass of unbroken scenery, Elias exclaimed, "Oh! Dad, doesn't that swaying green grass remind you of a lake with billowing waves?"

"It certainly does, son. I never have seen anything so beautiful."

Henry Whipple spoke up. "I believe this location is far more attractive than Baldwin's Prairie. I make a motion that we return to our camp and bring our families here."

"I second the motion," said Abraham Davidson.

"All in favor say aye, all opposed say nay," said Mr. Harrison. All four men said "aye".

"The ayes have it," said their leader. Everyone shouted and I believe Henry Whipple shouted the loudest. There was one added attraction they did not yet know about. This was to be a very happy surprise, but we will learn about that in another chapter.

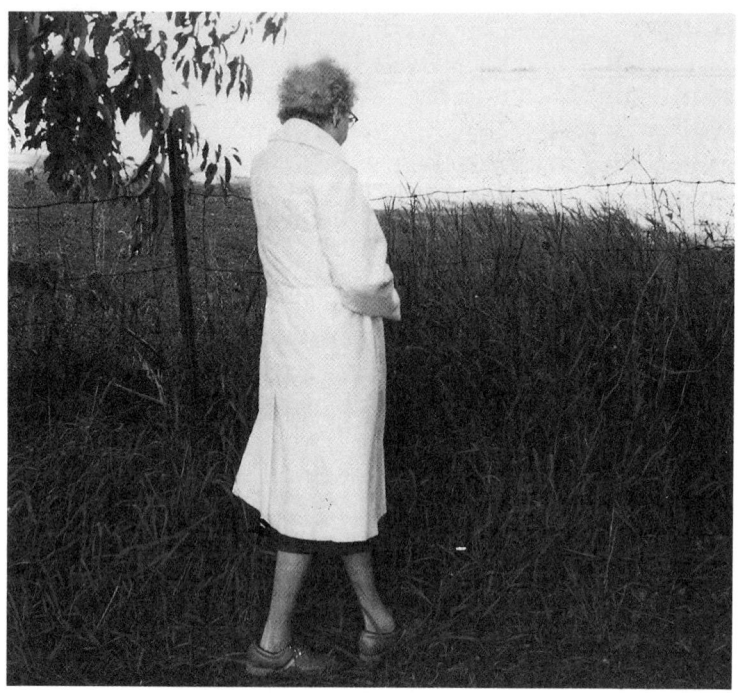

The tall prairie grass, called turkey foot or blue stem, confronted the Harrison party upon arriving in Michigan in 1828. Because its roots were embedded and intertwined under the ground it had to be pulled up by oxen, which were stronger than horses.

CHAPTER 36 - RIDING NON-STOP

It was with a great deal of enthusiasm that the spying scouts headed back to the dear ones they had left behind. It seemed as if the horses' feet hardly touched the ground, so eager were the riders to arrive home again to see their families. One would think they had entered a horse race. There was no stopping until they had reached the camp.

Almira was the first to see them coming down the road. She ran toward her mother shouting, "Here they come. Here comes Daddy and the other men."

The word spread like wild fire and soon everyone came running to meet the explorers. What excitement there was. Hugging and kissing took place as children jumped into their father's arms. Of course, the mothers did not want to be outdone by the children, so they ran to their husbands and were soon encircled by their loving embraces. Everyone was talking at once.

Finally, the excitement died down. Mr. Harrison shouted, "What's for dinner? Let's eat! I'm starved!"

Mrs. Harrison answered, "We sort of expected you so we cooked an especially nice dinner. Come on and eat. We can tell from your smiling faces that you have some very good news."

Plates were piled high with rabbit stew and

fresh corn bread that had been baked in a covered pan surrounded with hot coals. Flossie's fresh milk quenched their thirst.

The hungry scouts did justice to the good home cooking.

Elias said, "I think we all have lost about five pounds, but with this good food we will soon gain it all back."

"Martha and Worlenda," said Father Harrison, "just leave the dishes for a while and join us while we tell you about our experiences."

"Goody-goody," said his daughter. "We want to hear about your trip, too. Did you find the Promised Land?"

"We certainly did," said her father. "It is so beautiful and perfect I just can't describe it, but tomorrow we will pack everything and you will see for yourself in a few days. I am sure you will find it the most beautiful Promised Land anyone ever set eyes on. So have a good rest and good-night everyone!"

CHAPTER 37 - NEARING THE END
OF THE JOURNEY

As everyone prepared to retire for the night, there was a quiet peace in the camp. The tension and fears that had dominated the travelers seemed to melt away. For the first time in weeks, each member of the party was relaxed and enjoyed a night of sound sleep.

In the morning around the breakfast circle with the cheerful fire in the center, the topic of conversation centered around the trip north to their new home.

Mr. Harrison explained some of the reasons for deciding to move on instead of remaining at Baldwin's Prairie.

Breakfast consisted of bacon and eggs, corn bread with honey, topped off with more of Flossie's fresh milk. The hens, Crow, Crow Cackle and Spotty provided the eggs. One day's laying was not enough for so many people. Since the weather was cool, the eggs were collected each day and saved until there were enough for everyone. The hens and roosters rode in crates which were attached to the bottom of the Conestoga or in the wagons if there was room.

Happy families went about packing. Finally, everything was ready and our brave little party set off to seek new adventures.

As the wagons rolled along, one could hear the bleating of the sheep, the grunting of the

Ben Boden, the Bee Hunter, at work, as pictured in an 1881 edition of *Oak Openings*. Many believe Cooper used Bazil Harrison as a model for Boden.

swine, the crowing of the rooster, the mooing of the cows. The dogs were barking as they guided the animals. No doubt, the horses were doing their share of whinnying.

Eager eyes were peering from behind trees. They were astonished at the sight as some of the animals were new to them and the covered wagons were completely strange.

Loki, an Indian brave who stayed out of sight behind a tree, said to himself, "I will tell Sagamaw about white man." You see, Sagamaw was chief of the Potawatomies.

The noisy caravan had just reached the southern end of what was to be their new home.

Loki started off on the run, through the trees, so he wouldn't be seen by the newcomers. Panting and puffing, he arrived at Sagamaw's wigwam. He began in Indian language, "White man come, white boys, girls and squaws ride in..." Loki tried to say covered wagon with his arms. He decided to explain it by taking some green saplings and bending them to make a frame like that of the wagon. Then he put a cloth over it. He made noises like the animals. Sagamaw seemed to understand.

He said to Loki, "Tell braves to come here sun up." Loki knew that Sagamaw wanted his men to meet him the next day so they could welcome the white men.

He ran to the wigwams where the braves lived. He gave them the news. Sagamaw had also given orders for them to wear their gay powwow costumes and to paint their faces in bright colors.

The next morning the braves met Sagamaw in front of his wigwam. It was about eight o'clock when they had all assembled. The chief believed in law and order. He always chose two braves to walk with him as he led the rest three abreast. He was a fair and just leader, so he changed his companions every so often. His braves believed in him and appreciated his impartiality.

Today, they lined up and moved silently along the path to the camp of the first white settlers which was later to become the outlying community of Schoolcraft.

CHAPTER 38 - MR. HARRISON MEETS CHIEF SAGAMAW

It was November 15, 1828, when the noisy animals, four covered wagons, the huge Conestoga and 21 people suddenly discovered the greatest and loveliest prairie they had ever seen. Mr. Harrison and those with him were satisfied to look no farther, for perhaps the eye of man has rarely rested on a more beautiful natural landscape than was presented by Prairie Ronde.

Our friends found out later that the whole plain was covered from spring to autumn with a beautiful array of flowers whose differing colors followed each other in succession. These adventurers were so overwhelmed they remained speechless for a few moments while they stood drinking in the beauty.

Each member of the party had slept well and was feasting on a breakfast of fried potatoes and ham. They were rejoicing over and over again, but still the grown ups were not completely satisfied for had they not heard somewhere that a lake existed? But where was it? Oh! how they wanted to see a body of water which could make life easier for them.

Suddenly, "crackle, crackle," the twigs on the ground had been touched and here in this place where there was supposed to be practically no human life, what did they see?

Emerging from a thicket, twelve Indians

appeared. One of the twelve seemed to be the chief. He was unusually handsome. He had a big smile on his face and was wearing a headdress, which had bright feathers hanging down on each side of his head. The braves were wearing bands around their heads with a feather fastened at the back.

On one side of the chief were six braves and on the other side there were five. The Indians' clothes were of cotton cloth. Before traders came through the country, Indians wore clothes of skins. But, since they had been trading with the white man, they now wore clothes of cotton which they received from the traders in exchange for animal skins. The traders would ship these skins to foreign countries and make much money on them.

Thus, we can picture the Potawatomies wearing white men's clothes. However, they were dyed bright colors. Our friends noticed the gay costumes and the faces resplendent with paint. This attire they wore at their pow wows.

The tall Indian chief's name was Sagamaw. He was a very unusual chief and in a later chapter we will hear more about this important man.

As our Indian friends emerged from the thicket and stood side by side in a semicircle, Chief Sagamaw, with an outstretched hand, stepped forward and greeted Mr. Harrison with a hearty handshake. He had learned a few English words from traders and began to express himself the best he could. He said, "White man welcome." His good will and fine manner inspired confidence in our pale faced pioneers.

Now the all-absorbing question was where could water be found. So, with signs and a few Indian words which Mr. Harrison had learned from Elias, he was able to make Sagamaw understand their desire for water. Did they find water? The next chapter will tell us.

CHAPTER 39 - HARRISON LAKE

When Elias knew for sure that Sagamaw understood his father's desire to settle near a river, stream or lake, he said, "Dad, Sagamaw knows where there is water. He will lead the way."

Mr. Harrison gave the Indian chief a great big smile and patted him on the back. Sagamaw told his braves to line up three abreast. He made a gesture for our leader to join him. Elias said, "I guess I will go, too. You may need me to interpret."

Mr. Whipple decided he would go also. This left Ephraim Harrison and Ephraim Davidson to stay with the ladies and children. With the help of John and Bazel Junior, they would look after the livestock. Flossie and Lula Belle needed to be milked.

It was an impressive sight to see Mr. Harrison, age 57, and in the prime of life, walking next to Sagamaw, who appeared to be several years younger. They began to step out at a brisk pace. Elias and his brother-in-law, Henry Whipple, came behind and the eleven braves followed. They walked across the prairie to the northwest side of it. There they saw a small lake, beautiful and clear.

One brave walked with Sagamaw and Mr. Harrison, while one joined Henry Whipple and Elias. Mr. Harrison looked at Sagamaw and gave him another one of his engaging smiles. He pointed to his eyes then again pointed to the lake. He said, "lake" and Sagamaw repeated after him, "lake." This began a long and lasting friendship of these two people who could have been brothers. They were parallel in their gentle, upright, honest, dignified, and may I say, sophisticated manner. You will read in a later chapter the impression one of the future and later settlers had of this unusual chief.

The group of Indians escorted the new-comers back to their camp. Henry Whipple left the returning men to help those who stayed behind. They were trying to catch one of the hens that had decided to run away. The Indians laughed when they saw this.

Mr. Harrison and Elias took their new friends on a tour around the camp. When they came to an animal they would say its name. If it were a cow, Mr. Harrison would say "cow" and then have his class repeat after him, "cow." They learned several words this way. And in the days to come they would learn more. Mr. Harrison felt this would make his neighbors know he really cared for them and wanted to be kind to them.

When a cow began to moo, the Indians thought this was so funny that they lay on the grass while making the sound "moo." They laughed and laughed. Of course, our campers had a wonderful time laughing, too.

Time had gone quickly and everyone was hungry. The new friends must go back to their village.

Chief Sagamaw said a commanding word and his braves lined up in their regular fashion.

Mr. Harrison pointed to the lake and said, "lake" again. All the Indians said, "lake." Then he went one step farther and said, "Harrison Lake". They had trouble with the word Harrison, but because our teacher knew or understood good principles of teaching, they were soon saying "Harrison Lake" and today that body of water is still Harrison Lake.

For 46 days the members of our little colony had slept on the ground or on the hard wagon floors. Certainly it was time for them to think about building a place of protection. In the next chapter, you will read about how the Indians returned after dinner to offer their assistance in building a place of shelter.

After a hearty meal, Mr. Harrison said to his little group, "I feel we have come to our destination. We wanted to settle next to a body of water. What could be a better place than the lake we visited this morning? Let's break camp and make this location our next goal."

You can imagine the happiness and excitement which overwhelmed the eager travelers as they covered the last prairie on the last lap of the journey. As soon as the lake came into view, Bazel Junior began to shout, "We're here safe and sound."

After the wagons stopped, pandemonium broke loose. There was shouting, there was singing, there was jumping, there was clapping of hands and there was waving of arms.

Someone yelled, "Look at that beautiful, beautiful clear, clean lake. There are trees all around it. Some of them still have their colored leaves."

Abraham Davidson spoke up saying, "There are many trees on this side of the lake. Won't this be a lovely shady place for the log cabin? Then see the grass covered prairie stretching to the south. It seems to be surrounded by trees, but man alive, this flat land will make a wonderful place to plant our crops."

Mr. Harrison was happy because everyone agreed as to the beauty and the practicality of their property site, but he knew there was work to do. "Let's build our campsite," he said.

CHAPTER 40 - INDIANS TO THE RESCUE

Bazel Harrison, with his natural leadership ability, lost no time in organizing the work which must be immediately accomplished.

First, he decided where the log cabin should be. The wagons would have to be parked in an orderly fashion. Shelters and fences would have to be constructed for the animals. Trees would have to be chopped down to make the logs. These would have to be stripped of their bark.

Mr. Harrison hoped there would be stones available for the fireplace. Would there be clay on the property? This would be needed to hold the stones together. He was hoping a cement could be made to fill in the crevices between the logs. The cabin must be protected from the winter winds, which would soon be upon them.

As he was making his plans, he saw Sagamaw and his braves coming toward him. He was all smiles. He knew the white friends must have a log house. He had seen those of the traders and realized the white man lived in houses made of logs instead of wigwams.

Sagamaw had already suggested to his braves that they help with building the cabin and animal shelters. Of course, they had no argument about this and wanted to cooperate.

Sagamaw came to Mr.Harrison. He put his two pointer fingers together in the shape of a triangle. Then he pointed to the trees. He pre-

A typical blacksmith shop, much like the shop of Ephraim Harrison is shown.

tended he was chopping one down. Mr. Harrison smiled and let him know he understood. Sagamaw nodded his head. Mr. Harrison found a stone and made it known he needed stones for a fireplace. The Indians had seen the trader log cabins and stone fireplaces. They also knew that clay was needed to hold them together. The chief told a brave to find a clay pit which was on the property and bring some clay to him.

Sagamaw sent several braves to collect stones. The brave who had been ordered to find the clay ran right to the pit. He brought back a handful of the gooey stuff. Soon the Indians who were sent for stones returned with their arms full.

Was Mr. Harrison ever grateful for the help of the Indians! He knew he would have to provide buckets to carry the clay and the stones. He showed the Indians how grateful he was for what they had brought. He said "thank you" and pointed to the clay and stones. He had a great big smile. Sagamaw and the braves smiled, too. He said, "thank you" again. Soon all the Indians were saying the words "thank you."

Blacksmiths not only make shoes for horses hoofs, but they also make tools. Ephraim Harrison, who had been a blacksmith in Ohio, had brought all of his equipment with him. He thought other settlers would come with their horses and would need new shoes. When he saw the need for tools which the Indians could use, he came to his father and said, "Dad, let's count the axes we have and if we need more, I will make them."

"How much more can we be blessed," responded his father. "Our Heavenly Father has said He would supply our every need. Here we have stones, clay, wood and Indians to help us and now we can have extra tools. This is certainly a beautiful story, isn't it?"

"It certainly is," answered Ephraim. "Just wait until I tell Mother tonight. She will rejoice also."

This selection of blacksmith tools and artifacts includes ox shoes in the lower left.

A log cabin at the Kalamazoo Nature Center probably looks much like the one the Harrisons erected. Mrs. Harrison rejoiced because all of the materials needed to build the cabin were found on their property.

CHAPTER 41 - THE LOG CABIN

That evening, as the tired campers gathered around the blazing fire, our leader was jubilant. He could not wait to tell the members of the party how the Indians knew about the clay pit and where stones could be found. These resources were so very essential in building the log cabin's fireplace. He knew everyone would be happy to know about the desire of the Indians to help. In the devotional time that night, Mr. Harrison read Phillipians 4:19 and said to the group, "Our every need is being supplied."

As everyone left to retire, they knew that soon they would no longer be sleeping on the cold, hard ground or on hard boards, but on their beds, which would be brought in from the covered wagons. In order to accommodate all of the beds, Mr. Harrison realized they must build a loft with a ladder reaching up to it. Even if this was not enough space to take care of all the beds, at least the floor would be a luxury compared to what they were accustomed to. They could picture in their mind's eye that beautiful stone fireplace with a pot of stew bubbling over live coals.

Everyone slept like babies this first night. Oh, what peace they had. After breakfast the next morning, Mr. Harrison read Psalm 107:8 which really expressed their gratefulness.

About eight o'clock the men went to their wagons and found their tools for chopping down trees and stripping the bark. Ephraim Harrison was right there with his equipment to produce the correct tool.

Bazel Harrison had examined log cabins constructed by the traders so he knew just what to do.

Soon after they had started, the Indians arrived to help. It was not long before the men were chopping down trees. This had to be done first in order to make a clearing for the log cabin. A space 18 feet by 20 feet was reserved for it.

When enough logs were ready, they were notched at the ends so they would fit nicely on top of each other. There were no nails used. Bazel had learned to make cement using clay and gravel which was placed between the cracks of the logs to keep out the snow, wind and rain. Again, the Indians knew where they could find gravel.

The men had brought buckets to carry the clay. Both Bazel and the Indians had observed how the traders had made window panes of greased, dried deerskins. It may have taken a while before they were ready, but if it did, blankets could be placed over the openings until the skins were ready. Fortunately, winter was late in coming, so by the time it arrived the cabin was really snug and warm.

When Henry Whipple realized the small dimensions of the house, he said to Cynthia, "How does Dad expect 21 people to live in this small space? Let us take our wagon and move it some distance away. I don't believe I could ever live in this crowded condition."

"This is fine with me," agreed Cynthia. "I know the wagon will be colder than Dad's nice warm cabin, but I am a true pioneer and I am your wife. I am willing to do anything you say."

So, Mr. Whipple hitched his horses to their wagon and moved it about a quarter of a mile from the Harrisons. There, they put logs under each of the four sides as high as they could, leaving a space for a door. Then Cynthia placed blankets on the walls to keep out the wind and snow. The canvas cover, even though not very warm, was waterproof and, under the circumstances, the family survived this first winter. Perhaps Cynthia sometimes was tempted to say to herself, "If I had only known our expedition would turn out like this, I would have stayed in Ohio."

Her husband also expressed this feeling, but knew he could do nothing about it, so like a true explorer, he worked hard to provide wood for the fire and to make the best of things. The Indians kept them supplied with meat and Mrs. Harrison would say to her husband after they had finished a meal, "Dad, jump on Brownie and take Cynthia, Henry and the children what is left." Of course, Mrs. Harrison planned to have plenty left.

I am sure the Indians saw the need for collecting fire wood and the Whipples were grateful for their help.

As far as enough beds were concerned, I am sure if there were not enough to go around for the 16 people in the cabin, those rugged pioneers were grateful to sleep on the warm floor.

The log cabin fireplace was used for cooking, as well as being the heat source for the settlers. A handmade broom is leaning against the wall also.

Some fireplaces, such as this one at the Kalamazoo Nature Center, were made of clay, gravel and stones. Notice the tables and benches which were made of split logs with the smooth sides up.

CHAPTER 42 - THE NEW ICE BOX

After the cabin was finished, the next event was to unload the food which was still in the Conestoga. The Ohio neighbors had done an excellent job of labeling it to make it easy to sort out the needed foods while they were traveling. A great deal was left which could be used to feed empty stomachs for the rest of the winter.

Bazel realized that to prevent the remainder of the food from freezing, he must do something about storage. Before the floor was laid he said to his wife, "Martha, I believe I will dig out some of the dirt before we put in the floor. This will be a root cellar. We can have a trap door included in the floor, which will connect the cellar with the first floor. We can use a ladder each time we enter it. What do you think?"

"Dad," said Martha, "I feel this would be a wonderful idea. I was wondering how we could keep our vegetables and other foods from freezing."

So, with the help of Elias and Ephraim Harrison, Abraham and Ephraim Davidson, the root cellar became a reality. Of course, the Indians were there to do anything they could to help. They were given the tasks of carrying everything from the Conestoga to the cellar. Mr. Harrison placed it in an organized fashion so it could be easily found. The warmth from the floor heated by the fireplace would keep the food from

A rail fence was put around the animal shelters to prevent the animals from straying.

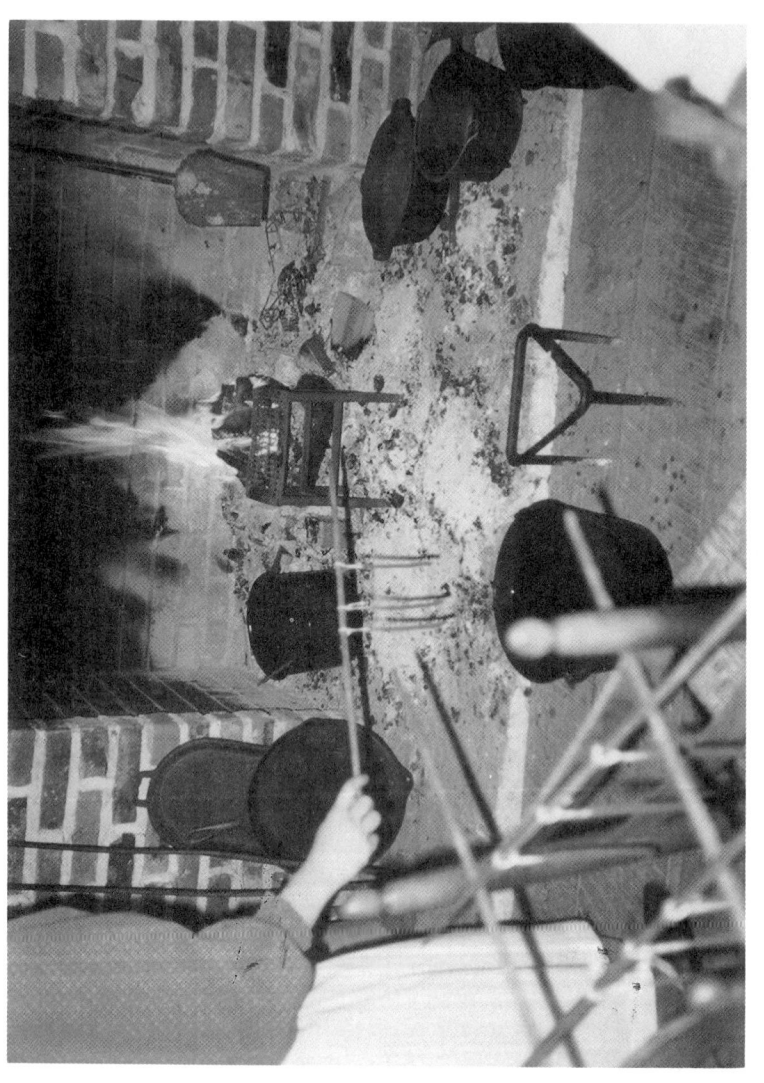

Candles dipped by Martha and Worlenda kept the family supplied with a source of light and were attractive additions to the fireplace mantle.

from freezing. If there was any danger, the trap door could be raised and the heat from the fireplace could take care of the problem.

In a few days, with the large numbers of helpers, including the Indians, the little cabin was finished. It even had four windows covered with greased deer skin. The fireplace was the big attraction. It was made of large stones cemented together with clay from the pits the Indians had found on the property. It even had a mantle which showed off Mrs. Harrison's lovely dishes and candle holders. Soon Worlenda and her sister, Martha would be dipping candles that would be placed in the candle holders. An iron bar made by Ephraim, the blacksmith, swung back and forth holding the big black kettle. Soon it would hold a bubbling stew made with meat which the Indians had given them. Vegetables from the root cellar would make it especially appetizing.

John and Bazel Junior were looking forward to catching fish in their own lake. How good they would taste frying in Mrs. Harrison's big black frying pan over the live coals.

The animals were snug in their corrals, made with branches and leaves to keep out the snow. Rail fences had been made to keep the animals from wandering away.

Of course, whenever anyone was hungry for pork or lamb chops, a pig or sheep would satisfy their hunger. Almira saw to it that Runty Grunty never met the fate of ending up on their dinner plates.

New beds were made by assembling the pieces in the loft as it would have been difficult to move them up the ladder after they were made. It seems as if pioneer beds were single ones so they could be moved easily from the first floor of the cabin during the day and stored in the wagons. The spinning wheel and loom were also stored and moved into the cabin only when they were being used.

A log cabin often had a loft to make sleeping space. It was much like a balcony, looking down to the main floor. Some had peg ladders as shown in this photo and others had regular ladders.

CHAPTER 43 - THE ICY PLUNGE

"Good morning, everyone," Bazel Harrison greeted his close friends and relatives as they sat around the fire eating breakfast. Usually his voice was strong and cheerful, but it had an air of sadness today as he sat down at the head of the table.

Mrs. Harrison spoke up, "Why, Dad," she said, "you sound as if you have a great problem. What is the trouble?"

"Yes," he replied, "I have just checked our food for the animals and our shelves are getting low. We have used it sparingly, but today I find it must be replaced. It has lasted through December, January and February and now in the beginning of March something must be done. The problem is that I must go to White Pigeon to replenish the supply. I have heard some traders tell about a settlement of about three buildings. One is a store and the other two are houses. The store has what we need."

"Why are you so sad then, Dad?" questioned Elias. "At least we can take the horses and wagon and go down there and buy enough supplies to last a while."

"Well, son, I wish this were all there was to it, but it so happens, according to the traders, there are no bridges and since it has become warmer, the ice which usually forms, has likely melted. To reach White Pigeon, it is necessary to cross the St. Joseph River. If I had known the condition of our supplies sooner we could have gone when the ice might have held us up, but now all we can do is ford the river. I will be the one to go. This trip will be very dangerous for both horses and myself. I realize that the current will be strong and the river will be high. Why, that current could sweep all of us right down to Lake Michigan. For tonight's devotions, I will read from Isaiah 43:2, 'When thou passest through the waters, I will be with thee; and through the rivers, they shall not overflow thee.' This verse will give us the faith we need."

That night the faith of this little band grew. They also realized what the cold water could do to both man and horses.

The next morning Bazel rose early and after a good warm breakfast, he hitched his strongest horses, Ben and Ned to a waterproof wagon.

The air was cool and crisp this early part of March. They finally reached the St. Joseph River. The water was high. Mr. Harrison knew he would have to remove his heavy outer clothing and place it in the wagon. He then drove Ben and Ned into the swirling water. He swam to their heads, grabbed their reins and guided them to the other side. Ice was floating around them. It seemed like an eternity during the time they were crossing. Mr. Harrison kept talking as much as possible to his horses, encouraging them to keep swimming. At this time his strong agile body was a great asset.

What a tragic event could have taken place right at this spot in the St. Joseph River. The author is pointing out the place where Mr. Harrison waded across the rushing water on that cold March day to go for supplies.

When they reached the opposite bank, the horses pulled the wagon up on dry ground. Mr. Harrison had brought some twigs and dry wood. Soon he and the horses were running around a roaring fire while his clothes were drying on nearby bushes. He put some food in a pan and as he continued to "exercise" around the fire, his clothes dried and his food cooked. After the horses were fed, he donned his outer heavier clothes and they were on their way. Every time the trail crossed the river, he had to repeat the process.

Finally, he arrived at White Pigeon where he received a royal welcome from those dear people. He remained all night and in the morning filled his wagon with supplies.

After completing this perilous journey, Bazel again reached his farm where he found a rejoicing group of people. "I hope I never have to go through this experience again," he said. And due to new settlers arriving who built a store, he never did. Of course, he planted crops and was soon able to provide his own supplies.

CHAPTER 44 - MARTHA HARRISON
PLAYS BABY SITTER

For whom did Mrs. Harrison baby sit? She was the first baby to live in the city of Kalamazoo, but she was not born in Kalamazoo. This is something like a riddle, isn't it? Do you want me to tell you about little baby Julia Bronson?

You see, her daddy was the first man to live in our city. His name was Titus Bronson. Everyone in Kalamazoo has heard the name Bronson because we have a park, a hospital and a street named after him. He named our city Bronson, but he did some things which the residents of our first city did not like, so they changed the name of Bronson to Kalamazoo. Perhaps it was because this was an Indian name and when these people moved here from far away states, there were many Indians living here.

Let's get started so we can find out why Mrs. Harrison was perhaps the first person to hold little baby Julia in her arms.

Mr. Bronson lived with his wife and little girl, Eliza, in Ohio. He heard from some traders that up in Michigan there was a place which had no settlers. There were only Indians.

"Mother," he said one day, "I would like to go to Michigan to see this place where they say there is a beautiful river and creek,"

"Then go," said Mrs. Bronson. So, Mr. Bronson walked all the way to what is now the

City of Kalamazoo. There were no trains, cars, buses or airplanes. He took his gun and some food.

At last he came to what we call the Kalamazoo River. He found a shallow place right by Riverside Cemetery. He walked across and went to what is now called Church and Water Streets. He built a log cabin and said, "Now I will go back to Ohio and bring Mrs. Bronson and Eliza with me."

After a number of days of walking, he arrived at his Ohio farm. He asked Mr. Richardson, Mrs. Bronson's brother, to come back with him to what would later be called Bronson. They brought as much as they could in addition to three oxen and a cow. Mrs. Bronson and Eliza rode in the wagon and Mr. Bronson and Mr. Richardson walked with the cow.

At last they reached the log cabin Mr. Bronson had built for his family. Eliza and her mother were very excited to see their new home. They arrived June 19, 1829. Everyone was busy. Mr. Richardson and Mr. Bronson hunted so they could have meat to eat. Mrs. Bronson spun some sheep's wool she brought with her. Then she wove it into cloth. Eliza learned to sew and knit stockings. But, remember, there were no other people except Indians.

But these dear people were getting lonesome. Now, Mr. Bronson had heard from some traders about the Harrisons who had come to Michigan the year before the Bronsons did.

What do you think Mr. Bronsons did?

Well, he just loaded Mrs. Bronson and Eliza into the wagon with blankets around them. Then he drove the oxen through the forest while Mr. Richardson led the cow. Soon they came to the Harrison log cabin beside Harrison Lake.

What do you think Mr. Harrison said when he saw four new people who he knew wanted to live with him? "Oh! Martha, why do those people have to come to stay with us? Don't we have enough mouths to feed? What will we do?"

No sir! He said nothing of the kind. He greeted them with a big smile and a hearty handshake.

"You are welcome here and we will gladly share what we have." He knew from their actions that they planned to move into the Harrison log cabin.

"We were so lonesome," said Mr. Bronson. Even though the Indians were good to us, we just wanted to visit some white people." This was in the fall of 1829. By this time, some of the Harrison children and neighbors had their own log cabins. Therefore, the sharing was not as big a problem as it would have been earlier.

Little Eliza wanted someone she could play with. I am sure she and Almira Harrison, who was now four, had many good times together, but she wanted a baby sister. Did she get her wish? She certainly did when one morning she heard, "wa, wa, wa," and there was Mrs. Harrison standing by the kitchen table. What was she doing? Why, she was holding a very little baby in her arms. Her name was Julia Bronson. Mrs. Bronson was in bed eating the breakfast Mrs. Harrison had prepared for her.

As soon as spring came and it was warm enough to travel with a tiny baby, the Bronsons said "good-by" to their kind neighbors.

Now there were several families living in and around Mr. Harrison's farm. About two miles from his home a little town sprang up, but the land around them was known as Prairie Ronde.

I wonder if the reason Mr. and Mrs. Bronson came to visit the Harrisons was because they were going to have a baby? Certainly, being alone as they were with no doctors or hospital near them might have something to do with it. What do you think?

CHAPTER 45 - NATHAN HARRISON'S DECISION

In this story, let us turn our time table back to the fall of 1828. Mr. Harrison was recruiting his family and neighbors to accompany him on his trip West.

He dropped in at his son's farm. Nathan was in the pigpen and had just finished feeding the pigs their field corn. What a noise they were making as they were oinking and devouring the corn.

"Nathan," said his father, "your mother and I have decided to pack up, sell out and go to Michigan. You are the last one to ask. How about it, son, would you and Anna like to come along with us?"

"Oh, Dad," said Nathan, "this is so sudden. We would have to think about it first. I have just started a new business and I would like to get on my feet financially. Perhaps in a couple of years we will be ready. I would like you to explain why you want to leave everything in Ohio and travel to that unknown area. You seem to be prosperous here. You are a good farmer and you are making money. Now do tell me why you would be planning such a perilous journey. You know as well as I all those dangers which will be lurking in your path.....no roads, only wolves and scalping Indians to confront you. Also, I hear that Michigan soil is hard and it is covered with swamps, infected with mosquitoes and full of malaria."

"Well, son, it is a long story, but to make it short, it is because the government and the war department have been trying to take my property. They wanted to give it to a soldier who fought in the War of 1812. Perhaps you remember how, at that time, we went to live on the William Henry Harrison estate. You know, he was a great general of that war. We went to live in his large house. We took over the farm and I worked it on shares. If I had not done this, no doubt, he would not have been able to serve in this high office.

"I felt in doing this that I was serving my country just as much as if I had gone to war myself. I even paid my brother, Ephraim, to go in my place.

"The War Department has told me three times that I must give my farm up to someone who did serve. Three times I have given a soldier seven hundred dollars, the price our farm was worth. This will make the fourth time I will have had to pay out that amount of money.

"Besides, Ohio is becoming too crowded with people and farms. I want to go to a place which has never been populated, where I can have all the land I want. To have a fresh start is my desire. I will take a chance on all those howling wolves, scalping Indians and mosquito infested swamps. I will let you know, Nathan, how we fare and after two years, if you wish to join us, our log cabin will be open to you. I hope this story is not boring as I have repeated it before to your other relatives."

"Thanks, Dad, you are very understanding," commented Nathan. Nathan worked hard. He prospered and at the end of the two years, he had saved enough money to go to Michigan. He sold his farm, his business and his live stock, except for two horses. He would use them to pull the covered wagon that he would need to transport himself, his wife Anna, some furniture and farm equipment. He also took two oxen, which were tethered to the rear of the wagon.

He started out having filled available space with supplies they might need on the way. By this time other Ohio citizens had the same idea, so he found the traveling conditions much better than those his father had met. He could manage with more narrow roads, since his covered wagon was smaller than his father's big Conestoga. Besides, he was not taking 50 sheep and 50 hogs.

In 1830 they arrived at Harrison Lake and were warmly greeted by their family and former neighbors. After a few days of visiting them and talking over the hardships they had encountered in traveling to Michigan, Nathan happened to meet a traveller who had just arrived from the little town of Bronson, which later came to be known as Kalamazoo.

"Greetings, friend," began Nathan, "just where have you been? You seem to know where you are going."

"Yes," answered the stranger. "I know where I've been and I do know where I'm going. I just came from Bronson, which is a little town about 20 miles from Schoolcraft. I am going back to my farm, which is located about two miles from here. I went to this little town to pick up my mail. Is there anything I can do for you?" asked the newcomer.

"Yes, " answered Nathan. "My wife and I just arrived a few days ago from Ohio. We are staying with my parents right now, but I am not satisfied to make Prairie Ronde our home. Do you have any suggestions?"

"I certainly do," said the man. "Bronson has a beautiful river known as the Kalamazoo running through its eastern end. This area would make an excellent location for you to settle. I believe there is some available land on its western bank."

In the next chapter, we will read about some exciting experiences Nathan encountered.

CHAPTER 46 - NATHAN HARRISON AND HIS NEW INVENTION

Let us call Nathan Harrison just Nate, as this is the name the settlers of Bronson used in speaking of him. Nate and Anna said, "good-by" to their relatives and friends who lived in Schoolcraft and at Harrison Lake.

When they arrived at Bronson in the spring of 1830 they went to the person who was selling land. You see, so far, the land office had not moved from White Pigeon. After learning of Nate's desire to buy land near the river, the salesman said, "We have one-half acre left which is at the juncture of a creek and the Kalamazoo River or, perhaps I should say that the creek flows into the big river." Later on this body of water was known as Portage Creek.

Nate bought the land for 75 cents as land was selling for $1.25 an acre. He drove his covered wagon along the road that later became East Main and finally Michigan Avenue.

Nate and Anna arrived about seven o'clock in the evening, just at the time when the setting sun was at its best. It filtered through spaces of the tall, beautiful trees, which lined the bank of the river. The sight of the sun's reflection made a rippling effect on the river. Nate and Anna were so awed by its beauty that they were spell bound.

"This is the place for us," said Nate to Anna. "Did you ever see such a beautiful scene in your life?"

"No, Nate," answered Anna, "this is God's handiwork."

As far as the author can determine, this spot was near the location of the present Mill Street Bridge, or it could have been closer to the river where the Michigan Avenue Bridge is located.

As the two were viewing the beautiful scene, they noticed two birch bark canoes, which were overturned and were leaning against the west bank of the river.

Nate commented to Anna, "We must realize that we have work to do and I am hungry. Let's come down to earth and make camp before it gets dark."

Soon a fire was made and they began to smell the aroma of the cooking food. Since they were not sure if it were safe to sleep outside, they slept in the wagon. After a good night's rest, they rose the next morning to make plans for their log cabin and the crops they would raise. Since it was still spring, they would be able to plant and harvest the result of their labors.

As they were looking toward the bank of the river they noticed two Potawatomi Indians, who turned the canoes right side up, pushed them into the river, jumped in and paddled away.

Later, Nate and Anna learned that these friendly Indians traded furs, venison and maple sugar for cloth, blankets and jewelry. They bartered with the settlers and traveling traders.

Nate and Anna built a small log cabin as simply and quickly as possible before they began to prepare the soil in order to plant crops. One morning soon after they were settled in their little home, they heard voices coming from across the river. There they saw a man, a lady, a little girl and a little boy emerge from a covered wagon. They went down to the river bank and stepped into the water. The lady and little girl lifted their dresses so they would not get their legs wet. The three of them proceeded to wade across as the father climbed back into the covered wagon. He began to drive the horses down the bank and splashed into the water. Nate and Anna had noticed the day before how this spot, with its shallow water, made an excellent fording place. The mother took the little girl by the hand and the boy tried to walk alone. The stony bottom began to hurt their feet. Once, the boy fell down. He came up dripping wet and crying. However, all three made the trip to the other side without further incident. The horses and wagon made it, but the west bank was so steep that the father had a difficult time driving them up onto the road.

As Nate and Anna watched this episode, they began to discuss this experience. "Surely," said Nate, "there should be an easier way for these settlers to cross this river. Anna, I am going to devise a plan. This can't go on in our front yard. Terrible things might happen, especially to the children. I did some wading yesterday and those stones are treacherous to the feet."

Nate began to think about what could be done to relieve the situation. Finally he came up with a plan. He would build a ferry or a barge. He had tools and equipment that he had brought from Ohio and decided to cut down some trees, split them in two and place the smooth sides up. He would fasten them together until it was long enough to hold a team of oxen or horses with a wagon attached. He would also make a pole that he could use to push the flat boat across to the other side of the river.

But, how would he get the people across? Nate remembered the birch bark canoes. He would ask the Indians, by gesturing, if they would trade them to him for something he had in his wagon. Sure enough, they agreed to make a trade! In the next chapter we will learn about how Nathan Harrison executed his plans.

CHAPTER 47 - NATHAN HARRISON AND HIS TOOTING HORN

Nate was making plans with Anna. "We will need the two canoes, since the families might have more than two children. After I take the ferry across, I could return to the east bank and help you with the transporting of the people, " explained Nate.

"Now we must decide on the fare we will charge. Let us ask four cents a piece for each animal and the wagon. For the people, I don't think six cents for each person would be too much. What do you think, Anna?"

"I think these prices are cheap enough," agreed his wife.

It so happened that Anna or Nate would see or hear the customers as they arrived on the opposite side of the river, but one day a problem came up. Both the Harrisons were so busy they failed to hear and see their customers. Anna came from the house and Nate appeared from the garden just in time to see a family use the ford in order to cross.

"Well, well," said Nate, excitedly, "Anna, we are going to lose business if this condition continues. We will have to do something to let them know we are here. I know what we will do. I have a plan!"

He went to the covered wagon and found a tin horn that he had brought from Ohio. He said to his wife, "I will make a sign that says,

'Toot the horn if you need service'." He found a tree which was right at the end of the Territorial Road, the road from Detroit and the one used by settlers from the East. He tied the horn on the tree and put the sign underneath it.

Nate thought, "Now we won't lose any more customers." You see, Nate Harrison had an eye for business and a knack for making money. One day Cyrus Lovell, an attorney who planned to follow this profession in Bronson, arrived on the opposite bank of the river. (By the way, Lovell Street was named after him). He saw the sign and thought to himself, "This is good business. I can be quite sure the owner of the ferry will come if I just blow the horn."

However, he was doomed to disappointment, when after giving some loud toots, he saw not a man appearing, but a lady carrying a basket. Soon he was to learn that in the basket was a new born baby. She put the basket on a stump and went to one of the canoes. She stepped in and paddled to the east bank. Mr. Lovell was there to meet her. She said in a sad voice, "Oh, dear! oh, dear! my husband is somewhere around, but I don't know where he has gone. My baby is only a few hours old. What am I going to do? I don't believe I can pole that big flat boat over to this side of the river. Where is Nate, Oh, where is that man?"

"My dear lady," said Cyrus Lovell, "you just let me take over. You see, I am an attorney and it is my profession to solve problems. You step in the canoe and I will take you back to your baby."

"You are very kind. By the way, what is your name?" asked Anna.

"My name is Cyrus Lovell and we came to Detroit from the State of New York via the Erie Canal."

Mr. Lovell took command and soon brought the flat boat to the east bank. He loaded his animals and wagon on it and took them across to the west bank. He then returned for his family and Anna. They rode in the canoe and soon everyone was safely on the other side.

Little Sunny, the new Harrison baby, slept through all the commotion. "Now, Mr. Lovell," said Anna, "since you did all the work, you owe us nothing. "

However, Mr. Lovell paid her a good sum saying, "This is rent money for your equipment. If I had not had it, we would have had to ford the river and I have heard it is difficult to do this. I am very grateful to you that you came at the sound of the horn. You are a very brave lady. I shall always remember you and if ever you need legal advice, look me up."

"I certainly will do that," said Anna.

I am sure that when Nate Harrison arrived from wherever he had been, he was much embarrassed to find out about what had happened. He apologized to Anna and told her this would never happen again.

CHAPTER 48 - OXEN TO THE RESCUE

It was in October of 1830. Mr. Merrit Cobb and his family arrived at the east bank of the Kalamazoo River. He had not heard about Nathan's ferry business, but he did know about the shallow place in the river, which he could use as a fording place. With this in mind, he drove his team of horses, which pulled his covered wagon, down into the water. But just as he almost reached the other side, the wagon became stuck in the mud.

Mrs. Cobb and the children waded across without too much trouble. But what was Mr. Cobb to do? No matter what he did the horses just got no where. They strained and strained, but the wagon would not budge.

So after everyone was on the west bank, Mr. Cobb said, "I guess there is nothing for us to do, but walk to Bronson. I have heard of a William Harris who lives right in the middle of town. Let's see if we can find him. Perhaps he will have some advice for us."

So the family began to walk. They were accustomed to this kind of exercise as this was the popular way to travel in those early days. They found Mr. Harris outside of his lean-to shanty, which was on the corner of what we know now as West Water and North Westnedge Streets. As they approached him, they began to smell food cooking over an open fire. Since they had not eaten anything since early morning, the

To make a scft, brown gel-like soap, the pioneers used a large kettle. Animal fat was saved and heated with lye, which had been made by allowing water to drain through straw and ashes.

tantalizing aroma of cooking food was most welcome. Right then, they paid no attention to Mr. Harris, but stood gazing at fresh fish and potatoes being fried to a golden brown. They were sizzling in a frying pan which lay on top of red hot coals. Nearby a black kettle hung from a tripod. In it they could see a mixture of boiling fresh vegetables which had just been picked from the garden.

Mr. Harris looked up from his culinary accomplishments and said, "Well, well, just where are you folks from and where are your horses and wagon?"

Without waiting for an answer, he plunged into an account of his cooking plans. "I am William Harris and I planned to prepare extra food which would last me for a few days, but I bet you folks are hungry. If that is the case, why don't you plan to eat your supper with me?"

"Oh, Mr. Harris," said Mr. Cobb, "you don't know how hungry we are and does that food look good. I could eat a horse."

"Then," said Mr. Harris, "why don't you freshen up? There is a pail of water on that three legged stool and on the ground is a washpan. You will find a fresh dish of brown homemade soap beside the pail. I made the soap out of grease and lye. I don't live very fancy out here in this wilderness. I suppose you are fresh from the cities in the East. You probably came by way of the Erie Canal. But, I know you are hungry. We can wait until after supper to hear all about you and why you are here. When you are ready, come over to my table, that I made out of split basswood logs. Put the pail of water on the ground and the misses can sit on the three legged stool to eat. Here is another one for you, Mister."

Mr. Harris had some knives and forks, an iron spoon and tin plates on which he could serve the food. The Cobbs could see that he lived up to his description "nothing fancy", but this was the least of their problems. In no time they had finished every fish, potato and vegetable. For dessert the host served corn bread that he had baked near the coals in a covered pan. For an extra treat, he served it with maple syrup.

Mr. Cobb began his story. "My name is Merritt Cobb and we came from Ann Arbor. As we were fording your Kalamazoo River, our wagon became stuck in the mud. The horses did their best to pull it out, but it wouldn't budge. We had to leave them right there. It's a good thing the weather is warm or they would catch a terrible cold. But, Mr. Harris, what are we going to do without our means of transportation? We were planning to go to Prairie Ronde to settle."

"Now, now," said their new friend, "don't worry one bit. I have an answer. You do what I say and your team and wagon will be right here in Bronson by tomorrow noon. You see, I have a friend whose name is Nathan Harrison. He lives right near where you were. It is strange you did

These oxen, named Lewis and Clark, belong to Jack Shoemaker of Tillers International, Portage, Michigan.

not see his log cabin."

"No, I guess I was too upset to look around," admitted Mr. Cobb.

"This is what I want you to do. Stay here tonight and in the morning leave your wife and children with me. You go back to the river. Look for a log cabin located on its bank. Go to the door and rap. When my friend appears you tell him all about your problem. He has a pair of oxen and I am sure he will loan them to you. Take them into the water and hitch them to your wagon. Those oxen of his are very strong and if you follow my directions, you will see what I mean."

So Mr. Cobb followed the advice of Mr. Harris and, of course, Nathan Harrison was delighted to make a new friend. The settlers called him Uncle Nate. He was so very friendly to everyone he met and made them feel welcome. It was not long before the horses and their wagon arrived at the center of Bronson. Of course, Mr. Cobb was very grateful to Mr. Harris and expressed his appreciation.

CHAPTER 49 - MR. HARRISON'S FERRY BUSINESS

As the ferry business grew and more people were coming from Detroit on the Territorial Road, Nate Harrison wondered where they had lived before. Some said they were from the State of New York. He knew New York was an eastern state, but the mystery was how could they arrive with their teams and covered wagons from a state that he knew was hundreds of miles from the Kalamazoo River. Sometimes he would hear them mention the city of Buffalo, Lake Erie and the Erie Canal. What did all this mean? He was determined to find out. Usually, there was not much time to ask questions while he was poling his ferry across the river.

But one day when he and Anna were bringing a family and their wagon and horses across the river, he said to the man, whose name was Fred Stone, "How would you like to stay for supper? You could park your wagon on our property, put your horses in our stable, eat with us, then perhaps you could answer some of my questions? You can camp in your wagon for the night, have breakfast tomorrow morning then, be on your way to Bronson?"

"Oh, I would like that very much," replied Mr. Stone.

After we learn something about the new bridge, we will rejoin Mr. Stone as he relates his experiences in answer to Nathan's questions.

Downtown Bronson Village during the great land boom. A photo of the mural which was located at the Kalamazoo Public Museum (courtesy of Michigan Bell.)

CHAPTER 50 - THE GREAT LAND BOOM

In 1835 the land office moved from White Pigeon to Bronson. At this time, it seemed as if word was spreading about the sale of land in Bronson, Schoolcraft, Berrien, Cass, St. Joseph, Branch and Calhoun Counties.

There was a great demand for land and Bronson was right in the midst of this boom. People were coming from everywhere. The land office was serving all of the above counties. In 1834, Bronson became a thriving town. All of the hotels were crowded and the eating places were packed. People were camping out. They were sleeping in the section that later became known as Bronson Park. In fact, they slept where ever there was available space. The traffic became so heavy a need for a bridge over the Kalamazoo River was apparent. Government officials offered to contribute $200 if the community of Bronson could raise another $200. Soon the money was provided and the bridge was built. Of course, Nate Harrison was put out of business. However, he had learned to be quite a businessman. Even before this boom, he had built a hotel and eating place which he operated along with his ferry business. No doubt, Anna Harrison had a great deal of fortitude and business ability which she developed while helping her husband run the ferry. She must have taken responsibility for managing the new hotel.

BUILT IN 1833

The sizable Kalamazoo House was built at the corner of Michigan and Portage streets by Gen. Justice Burdick at the same time that Nathan Harrison built his River House near what is now a golf course on King Highway.

The bridge was finished in about 1837 and Nathan's River House Hotel began to prosper during the land boom. By the way, the street known as Harrison was named in honor of his achievements. For some time, Nathan's hotel competed with Justus Burdick's Kalamazoo House, which operates today as a Bed and Breakfast on South Street.

The height of the boom came in 1836 when the local land office disposed of 1,634,511 acres. More land was sold that year in Kalamazoo than in any other land office in the country. The total receipts amounted to $2,043,866.87. In 1836 the town's name was changed from Bronson to Kalamazoo.

The land boom ended when President Andrew Jackson required that all land purchased from the Federal Government had to be paid for in silver or gold. Prior to this, bank notes were accepted.

When the land office moved to Bronson from White Pigeon in 1835, the town's first newspaper was established. In 1833 it was known as the *Michigan Statesman* and *St. Joseph Chronicle*.

No doubt, the newspaper's owner, Henry Gilbert, was attracted to the printing business provided by the land office. He continued to publish his weekly newspaper under the title of the *Michigan Statesman*. The first issue was printed October 2, 1835. In 1837 the name was changed to the *Kalamazoo Gazette*. This paper is

Kalamazoo's founder Titus Bronson as painted by Benjamin Cooley in 1870 (courtesy Kalamazoo Public Museum).

the oldest in the State of Michigan, except for that of Detroit.

Titus Bronson became perturbed because the state legislature, approved by Governor Mason, changed the name of the town from Bronson to Kalamazoo. He was quite an eccentric person who had peculiar habits. Consequently, several men who owned extensive property in the village used their influence in changing its name. Bronson was unhappy about this and moved away.

In the next chapter, we will find the answer to Nate Harrison's question as to how the pioneers from the eastern states could arrive in Michigan without facing the hardships his father and other settlers encountered as they drove their covered wagons and Conestogas many, many miles across the land.

CHAPTER 51 - MR. STONE BEGINS HIS STORY

In the evening, the Nathan Harrisons entertained the Stones for supper, after which the children were put to bed. The adults were seated outdoors around a blazing fire. When everyone was comfortable, Nathan said, "We are indeed grateful that you friends are willing to give us your time in explaining this question about which I have pondered for such a long time. How does it happen that you had such an easy trip coming to Michigan, while my father and I and many others achieved our dreams by facing hardships, such as fighting off howling wolves, making our roads, traveling around swamps, hunting for water and animals that could supply us with meat?"

"Yes, Mr. Harrison," commented Mr. Stone, "I think we are the ones to be grateful for your friendship, hospitality and this delicious meal. Whenever you are ready, I am only too happy to try to answer your questions."

"Anytime you wish to begin, we are most ready to listen to your account," answered Nate Harrison.

"You see, friends, we had some things going for us. We had the Erie Canal in our favor. We had heard about it as it was a much talked about feat of engineering. It was finished in 1825 and was a great boon to traveling. We began to ask questions of our friends and neighbors and discovered that Troy, New York, a town near us, was on the canal's route. If we made a trip to Troy, we could receive the information we needed about the price of tickets and the time the barges arrived.

"Mother and I left the children with a neighbor and set out on our new venture. When we arrived in Troy, we received directions as to the location of the family that ran the canal business. We had no trouble finding Mr. Brown, the owner.

"He understood why we had come and soon was explaining everything we needed to know about traveling West.

"He began his informative speech saying, 'I believe you friends are here to find out how you can go to Michigan with the greatest of ease. No fighting the elements like our neighbors from other states are doing.

" 'First of all, Mr. Stone, after you have sold your farm you will need to purchase a covered wagon. Buy one that requires two horses to pull it. No doubt you have them already. If you want to take your dog, you may do so, but it will be placed with the other animals. You may exercise your pet as often as you wish. Put in your wagon the items you will need when you start housekeeping in Michigan. It is not necessary to bring any food for the canal trip as we have experienced chefs who will cook and serve the meals. When you arrive in Detroit, you can stock up on supplies. The steamer that will take you from Buffalo to Detroit will also serve your meals. As soon as you sell your farm and are ready to leave, let me know and I will make a reservation for your family and animals.'

"Mr. Brown was a very busy man so I did not ask any more questions. There were many things I wanted to know, but I knew the events that would take place on the barges would have to come as a surprise. For several days, we had been packing the covered wagon with the things we knew we would need when we arrived in Michigan. We had learned to love our neighbors so much that when the day came to leave, we were very sad.

"Knowing that money would be needed to pay our fare on both the barges and on the steamer, we had been saving for quite some time. Also, we would have to buy land and have enough to supply our needs until we could begin farming again.

"Arriving in Troy, we went straight to the canal station. Other families were also waiting with their covered wagons, oxen and horses. Of course, we had faith that Mr. Brown knew what he was doing. But questions were running through my mind as to where the wagons and animals were to be placed. Soon we heard a ringing bell in the distance. One of the two barges appeared, being towed by two horses. A boy was sitting on a third horse. Evidently, it was his task to drive the other two, which were walking in single file. These horses were soon replaced with fresh ones.

"We were curious to see just what would happen next. The first barge came close to the canal bank and was anchored to a stake by a deck hand. Several other men approached. They unhitched the horses from the wagons. A ramp was placed from the bank to the lower part of the barge and soon the horses were being led into this section, which would be their home during the trip. Now what were they going to do with the wagons, I wondered. The deck hands removed the wheels and the next thing we could see, they were being hoisted by pulleys right up to the upper deck. Those men must have been strong, because working as a team, they were able to park them on the top of the barge deck. We wondered why the wheels were removed, but later learned that if a strong wind came up the wagons could be blown off the roof.

"Now I will explain what happened to us."

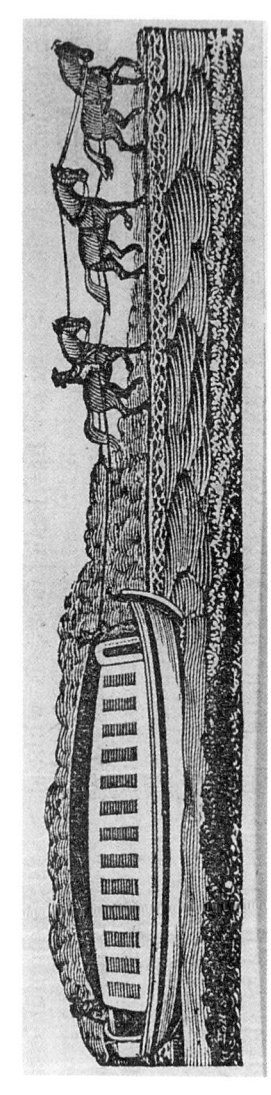

Erie Canal boats like this carried thousands of immigrants across New York state to Buffalo where they embarked on vessels to sail across Lake Erie to Detroit and a new life in "Michigania."

CHAPTER 52 - A CANAL HOLIDAY

Mr. Stone continued his story by saying, "After the animals and wagons were stored away in the first barge, a man appeared who was to be our host. He said, 'Ladies and gentlemen, you are about to embark on a carefree ride on our newly invented Erie Canal barge. I shall be your host captain. My name is Hezekiah Carnes. You don't have to call me by name, just say Cappy and I will be at your service. After the barges start, I will give you some information about this beautiful idea of moving you New Yorkers to Michigan in a way you will enjoy as a holiday.'

" 'For most of the time, the weather cooperating in giving us warm and sunny days, you will be sitting or standing on the deck. You will enjoy beautiful scenery. First of all, we will examine the lower floor. Follow me and I will give you some instructions.' As a group, we followed Cappy down a few steps and entered what was to be our dining room, our sleeping quarters and, if it rained, our living room.

"He continued. 'I wish to introduce you to Jim Knight, who is standing here. He will be your porter. He will assign you to your private areas. Your sleeping quarters will consist of berths that will be placed on each side of the barge. Jim will make these up at night and take them down in the morning. The ladies and children will sleep in the forward part of the barge, while the men will occupy the rear. A red curtain will be your partition. At six o'clock, you will meet back here where tables will be set for the evening meal.'

"A bell rang at 6 o'clock and we came down from the deck to eat. We were served by colored waiters, who tried to make our meals pleasant. We had an enjoyable evening, riding under a bright moon. We told stories, sang songs and had a good time until bedtime. When we entered the main room, we saw the berths were made up. After a good night's sleep, a bell rang at six in the morning. We dressed, after which Jim took down the berths and put the tables together for breakfast. We followed this routine until we arrived at Buffalo. I might say our trip was certainly a holiday as we were waited on hand and foot by those pleasant and courteous black people.

"One of the evenings was spent listening to Cappy give us considerable information about the building and mechanics of the canal. This particular evening, the ladies and children were seated on chairs and benches on the upper deck. They were dressed in their gingham dresses with matching sun bonnets. One lady was carrying a parasol, which she used to protect her skin from the sun. The men were dressed in their stylish suits and were wearing stove pipe hats. Some of them were standing and some were also seated.

"Cappy came up on the deck and began, 'How would you passengers like to know something about the history of this canal and some basic facts regarding it?'

"I told him that I was dying to know how all this wonderful invention started and all about the little details he could give us. The other passengers clapped their hands, so Cappy knew he would have an attentive audience.

"He began his story, 'You see, there was a great need for a waterway to connect the city of New York and other cities along the Hudson River with the West. That meant a canal should be dug from Albany to Buffalo.'

" 'In 1810, some of the businessmen of New York City stimulated Mayor DeWitt Clinton to appeal to the United States Government to furnish money for such a project. He and Gouverneur Morris travelled to Washington with no results. The answer was that the whole project was foolish and unprofitable!'

" 'However, when election time came to choose a new governor, Mr. Clinton ran for office on the platform of building the Erie Canal. He won the election and plans began for its construction. It was finished and in 1825, a celebration took place. A barge carrying important dignitaries left Buffalo, New York, with a barrel of Lake Erie water. When it arrived in New York Harbor, Governor Clinton, ceremoniously, poured the water into the New York Harbor.'

" 'This project has proven very profitable. It opened a way for manufactured goods to be transported to the western states and to carry raw products to the East. Of course, it will probably make New York a very large city. Now I will relate some details which may interest you. The canal is 363 miles long, starting from the Hudson River and arriving at Buffalo. The trotting horses can pull the barges one and one-half miles an hour. The charge per mile is one and one-half cents. The canal is 40 feet wide at the surface and tapers to 28 feet at the bottom. It is also four feet deep.'

" 'You will soon be coming to bridges and as we go under them the guide will tell us to duck our heads so they won't be chopped off.

" 'When you come to the locks, no doubt you will receive more information on them. This is all for tonight, because when I start on the subject, it is hard for me to quit. If you have any questions, I will try to answer them.'

"I thanked Cappy and told him I appreciated all of the information he gave us.

"When we arrived at Buffalo, the barges were anchored to a dock. We were wondering how the deck hands would take care of the wagons and animals. We didn't have a long time to wait as we saw them bringing the wagons down from the barge's roof. Then, they brought the animals up on the dock. In no time at all, every horse or ox was hitched to its own wagon, which now had its wheels in place.

"The deck hands were calling out the names of the owners. When my name was called

I went over and claimed my wagon. Mother and the children followed as we didn't have far to walk to our waiting steamer.

"After riding on that small barge, the steamer looked like a castle. More deck hands were waiting to take care of our wagons and animals. We drove them down into the lower part of the ship where wagons were parked and the animals were taken to their stalls. Guides told us where we were to go. Soon we found ourselves in a spacious room, which was to be the steamer's dining room. We were then shown our sleeping quarters and told we could go on the upper deck until lunch was ready. The weather on Lake Erie was perfect and after several days, we landed in Detroit.

"Again we claimed our horses and wagon. After stocking up with supplies we would need for the trip on the Territorial Road, we found ourselves a few days later at your Kalamazoo River. So, Mr. and Mrs. Harrison, this is all I have to say. But you can now see how thankful we were that we had saved enough money to come the easy way to your Michigan."

"Thank you so very much for your story, Fred. Just call us Anna and Nate. I feel as if we are a family and no longer strangers," replied Nate.

CHAPTER 53 - JUDGE HARRISON ACTS ON BEHALF OF WHITE FEATHER

It was October 17, 1831. Governor Cass had just commissioned Bazel Harrison and Stephen Hoyt to be associate judges of the district that would one day become Kalamazoo County. This term of office lasted until sometime in 1834. During his tenure, Judge Harrison made many decisions regarding legal cases. Everyone felt that his decisions were fair. We can see from the following story that the Judge practiced a great deal of wisdom in deciding them.

Let us go to his farm. He had just left the barn and was walking up the road to his log cabin when he saw someone enter the drive. He decided it was his Indian friend, White Feather, who had a great deal of respect for the Judge. He had learned some English and could communicate to some extent with the Prairie Ronde settlers.

Judge Harrison noticed that White Feather appeared to be somewhat agitated and was mumbling to himself. He said, "White man tooked horse. No like white man."

Just then the Judge met him face to face. "Where horse?" he asked.

"White man tooked horse," answered White Feather.

"Time to eat," said the Judge. "Come to the cabin and have breakfast."

The two men walked arm in arm to the front door that faced the lake. You see, his front door was placed so he would be able to have a good view of his beautiful lake. The two men entered. Mrs. Harrison had just sliced off pieces of corn meal mush and they were sizzling in pork fat. When they were beautifully brown, she served them with wild honey the Judge had collected the day before.

Did White Feather have a feast? He ate and ate and Martha Harrison fried and fried more pieces of mush. When they finished eating, the Judge told Martha not to wait lunch at noon for him as he and White Feather planned to go on some legal business.

He found Brownie and the two men mounted him. On the way White Feather described the man he thought might have stolen his horse. He also said, "Horse white spot on nose".

Judge Harrison thought the description of the thief to be that of Josiah Long John. When Brownie came near the Long John farm, the Judge said to his friend, "Jump down from Brownie's back and hide in those bushes. I will be back soon."

White Feather followed the Judge's directions. After a few minutes, Brownie came galloping into the Long John drive. As he did so, Mr. Harrison saw some horses eating grass in a nearby field. There he saw one with a white spot on his nose. As Brownie came up the drive,

Mr. Long John came out of his house.

"Hello, friend," said the Judge. "You have a mighty fine looking horse in your field, the one with the white spot. I certainly would like one like him. He looks as if he came from good stock. Perhaps he has a brother or sister I could buy. Where did you get him?"

"I bought him from Charles Rhodes who lives a little way from me." answered Josiah Long John.

"Jump on my horse. I want you to go with me. Perhaps you can describe him better than I can. The two men mounted Brownie and soon they came to Charles Rhodes' farm. He was outside feeding his chickens. When Mr. Rhodes saw them he said, "Well, well, if it isn't Judge Harrison and Josiah Long John. Is there anything I can do for you two neighbors?"

"There certainly is," said the Judge. "You see, neighbor Long John has a horse he said he bought from you and I thought you might have one that came from the same stock. If you do, I would consider buying him.

"Now, now," said Charles, "you know, Josiah Long John, you did not buy that horse from me."

Judge Harrison did not want to embarrass Josiah in front of Charles Rhodes and he wanted to be diplomatic in this case. So he said, "Perhaps you will think of the person you did buy the horse from after we mount Brownie. Maybe, Josiah, you have a case of being absent minded, like we all get at some period in our lives!"

The two men jumped on Brownie's back. On the way to the Long John farm Josiah said, "Judge, I took White Feather's horse and I am very sorry. I will never steal from anyone again, I promise. I need to turn my life around and be an honest, kind man like you. Thank you for being so patient with me."

"Since you feel as you do, Josiah, I shall not make you pay a fine this time, but if ever you get in trouble with the law again, you may find yourself in real trouble," commented the Judge.

When the two men parted, they shook hands.

This story is just an example of the wisdom Judge Harrison used in deciding his legal cases. It was commonly known that he would sometimes ride all day for the purpose of bringing about an amicable settlement in a difference between neighbors.

Usually one thinks of a chief justice as being a learned student of the law, but Judge Harrison "required small aid from the lore of the law to enable him to render substantial and satisfactory justice in the cases his neighbors brought before him. He was always spoken of with respect, and as his humble cabin by the lake was a landmark on the prairie, so was he always prominent and noted among his fellow pioneers." (from Stone).

CHAPTER 54 - THE FIRST SCHOOL

By 1830 the population of Prairie Ronde was increasing to the extent that a one room school was needed. Families were coming in covered wagons from Ohio, Indiana and the states on the eastern coast.

The first schools were made of logs, but as sawmills were becoming popular, these schools were made of sawed boards and became known as "the little red school houses."

A school which was probably made of logs was erected at Insley's Corners. This school lasted during the winter months from 1830 to 1831. Another one was established at Harrison Corners in the winter of 1831 and 1832.

No doubt, when Almira was old enough to attend school, she went to one near her home. We will push ahead to the year of 1836. Almira Harrison was eleven by now and was probably in the fourth grade.

Up to this time, John and Martha had used the books they had brought with them from Ohio. The school provided some and the other students had brought theirs from the states where they had lived. The books which were furnished by the school were old and new books were hard to come by.

Usually, Almira was a cooperative and model student, but all of a sudden, she lost all interest in school. It was in September of 1836. Almira had just finished breakfast. "Daddy," she said, "I don't want to go to school today."

"Well, well," answered her father, "why don't you want to go? Are you not feeling well?"

"Yes, Daddy, I feel all right. But I am sick and tired of the same reading books. I have read them so many times I know them all by heart. I wish we could have some new ones."

"Yes, honey, I would feel the same as you do if I were in your place. But I may have good news for you. I saw your teacher, Miss White, at Huston's store last night and what do you think she told me?"

"Oh! Daddy, I don't know. Please tell me."

"Well, honey," answered her father, "there are some boxes at the Bronson Post Office. They contain a surprise for you students."

"Oh! goody, goody," said Almira. "Are you going to Bronson to pick them up?"

"That's just what Miss White suggested I do. She also said, "I will ask all of the students to invite their parents to come to a meeting on Monday night. You children are invited too."

"Will we open the boxes at this time?" questioned Almira.

"We certainly will do that," answered her father.

Since Mr. Harrison knew there were three boxes waiting at the Bronson Post Office for the Prairie Ronde School Number Two, he harnessed Ned to his wagon. He was not sure if the boxes would be too big to fit on Brownie's back, so he felt the wagon would be the best way to transport them to the school. When he arrived, it was recess time and Miss White had the children interested in playing a game outside. Consequently, they did not see him carry the boxes from the wagon to the school house. He placed them under Miss White's desk and put a coat on top of them. If the children suspected there was something hidden there, they never said a word.

Down deep in everyone's heart, excitement was reigning. Finally, six forty-five Monday night came. The parents and children were sitting on seats which were made of long boards laid across some short tree stumps.

Miss White's desk was made higher by placing boards on higher tree stumps.

Mr. Harrison, who was active in community affairs, was chosen to open the boxes. At seven o'clock Miss White stood in front of everyone and said, "I want you to listen to a story about a little boy. Then when we open the boxes hidden under my desk, I'm sure the contents will be more greatly appreciated. A letter came to me with one of the boxes. In the letter there is a story about William McGuffey."

All eyes were riveted on Miss White and each person was as still as a mouse.

"You know, boys and girls," she began to read, "little William was born in 1800 in Clay, Pennsylvania, which is on the East Coast. His family was very poor and in order to attend school they would have to pay his way. Mother

Almira and her niece are ready to go to bed. Almira has been reading her *McGuffy Reader* and studying her spelling words by writing them on a slate.

McGuffey taught him his ABC's, but she did not have time or didn't know how to teach him to read.

"When William was six years old, he said, 'Mother, I want to go to school so much I think we should pray for the money to pay the school.'

" 'William,' she said, 'let's ask God every morning in our prayer time that some way He would send someone who will pay for you to go to school.'

"So, every morning Mrs. McGuffey would kneel by a kitchen chair next to an open window. One day something wonderful happened. A preacher who happened to be going by the house heard Mrs. McGuffey earnestly praying for the education of her children.

"Little Willie watched the children as they walked by his house, talking and laughing. How he wished he could attend school.

"He did not see a preacher as he entered the McGuffy home. Suddenly, he heard his mother call to him.

"Mrs. McGuffy explained to Willie that he would now be going to school as a kind man said he would pay his way.

"Soon, little Willie was attending Old Stone Academy at Darlington, Pennsylvania and this kind and sharing preacher paid his way. This was in 1807. When William finished the academy, he worked his way through Washington and Jefferson College. He was so intelligent that he could easily learn ancient languages such as Latin and Greek. He became a professor of those languages when he was only 26 years old. He then began to write the books we will soon be looking at. Just think, he did all this in just ten years, as this year is 1836.

"You boys and girls have been so very quiet while I have told you this story. Now I believe we should do one more thing before Judge Harrison opens the boxes. Let's thank God for William McGuffey and Mrs. McGuffey's faith. Then let's thank Him for the preacher who paid his way to Stone Academy."

After Miss White finished her beautiful prayer of thanks, she said to Judge Harrison, "It is your turn now, Judge. Go to it."

Can you imagine how long it took him to open the boxes? He had those books out of their cases before you could say "Jack Robinson".

Perhaps you can imagine how happy everyone was. All restraint went out the window as each beautiful book was carefully taken out and placed on Miss White's desk. The little children grabbed the primers and McGuffey first grade readers. The middle sized children were running around carrying the McGuffey second grade readers. The fourth and fifth graders picked up their books, hugging them tightly in their arms. The sixth graders were doing the same with theirs.

What a hub-bub these children were making as they ran to their parents to show

An authentic writing slate used around 1835 is displayed at Colby Long Cabin, Benton Harbor, Michigan.

them these shiny, beautiful books. Even the paper in them had a clean and fresh odor.

The parents were rejoicing and exclaiming along with the children as to how inviting and tempting the books were.

Finally, Miss White picked up her long handled bell and rang it. When everyone was quiet, she said, "It's time for refreshments. Come over to the table to see what Mrs. Harrison has brought to us." There they saw one of her famous Johnny cakes and beside it was a pitcher of fresh wild honey, which Judge Harrison had recently collected.

Everyone had such a good time and the children were saying, "I can't wait to start reading my books." The parents were very glad they had contributed to the purchasing of them.

CHAPTER 55 - ALMIRA THE WRITER

The next day when the children returned to school, they were very eager to read their brand new books. Almira especially loved them. She said to Miss White, "I would like to read all of the books up to the fourth grade reader. I will keep this one to read only in class. After I do this, I would like to write some stories for my sister Cynthia's children."

"Oh! Almira," said Miss White, "I think this would be wonderful. To think you would be writing your own stories. To make it easier, I happened to buy some new paper which came from the East. Mr. Houston just received a new shipment. I will help you with your materials to write the stories. Our turkey quill pens are a little dull, but I will sharpen them and make some new ink for you. I found some fresh berries on the way to school. They will make excellent ink."

"Thank you, Miss White," said Almira. After she had finished reading the third grade reader, she looked for a story she could rewrite. There it was. It was called *The Insolent Boy*.

So Almira said to Miss White, "I found a good story which I want to write. Look, it is on page 15."

"Yes, Almira," said Miss White, "I have been reading the readers, too, and I like that story."

Almira began her story.

Mother Harrison waves goodbye to Almira as she leaves for school carrying her *McGuffy Reader.* Julie Sherfield plays the part of Almira.

"In a little village there lived a father, a mother and a little girl named Caroline, who had a brother named James. Now James Felton will be the subject of our story. He was a very insolent boy. When he walked down the streets of this little town where he lived, he would be mean to anyone he saw. However, he did not do anything which really hurt them, so no one felt like telling his parents. But one day something happened which really made James change his ways. He and his schoolmates had just left school for the day. They were walking along the street when a stranger appeared. He was wearing a black suit and a black broad brimmed hat. Over his shoulder was a cane and at the end of the cane was a bag. When James saw the newcomer, he ran to him and grabbed his hat. He threw it on the ground, then ran away. The man picked it up and put it back on his head.

"James ran back to see if he could do further mischief, but just as he came close, the man grabbed his arm and held him tightly. When the man was holding him, he told him that he had bad manners and was very rude and that he better change his ways. James ran a little distance; he took a piece of hard brick from his pocket and threw it. The brick hit the man over his eye and left a wound. Then James stopped to talk to his classmates who were watching him. The man started to walk on and after James had talked with the boys a few minutes, he walked across a field and was soon home. When he came to his house, Caroline was outside.

" 'Oh! James,' she said, 'Uncle David just arrived. He has been traveling and has brought all of us some beautiful presents and just think, he has a gold watch on a chain for you. He has a wound over his eye. Mother put a bandage on it. He wanted to surprise us so he left his carriage at a farm outside of our village and walked the rest of the way.'

"James became very frightened and ran into the house. He went to his room and hid. When his father realized that his son was upstairs, he called, 'James, come down and meet your uncle.' But James was too frightened to meet his uncle. Finally he knew he must go downstairs. His mother met him and said, 'James, you are not like this as a rule. What has happened?'

"But James could only hang his head. As he entered the living room, he kept his eyes closed and would not look up. When the man saw him, he said to his brother, 'This is not your son, this is the boy who threw a brick at my head. I have brought some beautiful presents for all of you. I have a gold watch on a chain for James.'

" 'Oh, no,' said Mr. Felton. 'Don't give him any presents. He will have to learn how to behave.' And James had to go without his lovely gold watch. He never did receive it! But, from that time on, James learned his lesson. He was always kind and polite and tried to help people to be happy. The villagers were surprised to see the wonderful change that had come over him."

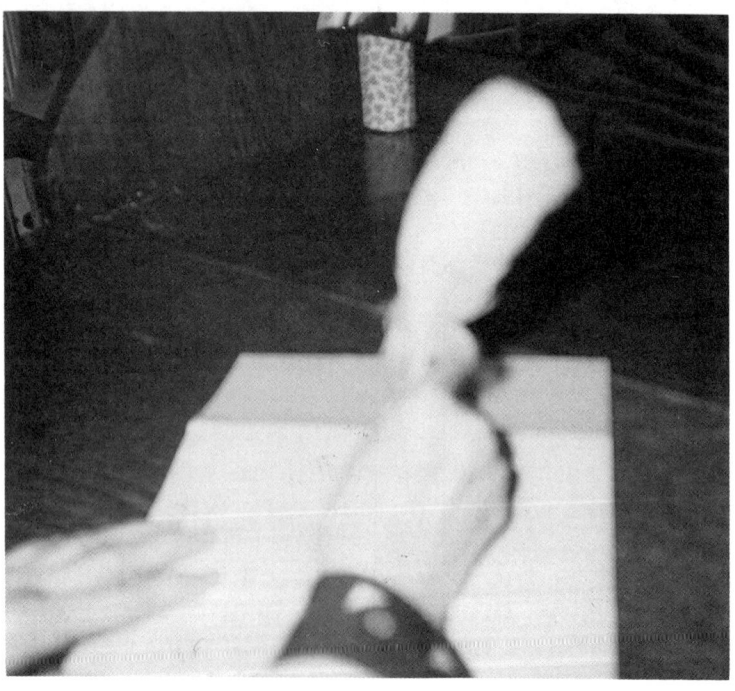

Miss White sharpened Almira's turkey quill pen and made new ink out of fresh berries she found on the way to school. The picture was taken at the Celery Flats Festival in Portage, Michigan.

CHAPTER 56 - BEAUTIFUL HANDS

The next day, Almira said to Miss White, "I finished my story called *The Insolent Boy*. Is it all right for me to write another one?"

"It certainly is," answered Miss White. "You not only plan to write your stories, but I think you are intending to read them out loud to your nieces and nephew. Is this correct, Almira?"

"It certainly is and I probably will write about each story in our new McGuffey Readers."

Almira began her next story this way, "Once there was a little girl named Daisy Marvin. In her school there was another student named Mary Jessup. One afternoon Daisy Marvin stayed after school. She said to Miss Roberts, her teacher, 'I would like to remain in the school room until you are ready to leave.'

"It so happened that Daisy didn't live too far from school and her home was on the road which led to that of Miss Roberts. When she had finished her after school duties, Miss Roberts said to Daisy, 'I guess I'm ready now, so let's start for our homes.'

"As the two walked along, Daisy said to Miss Roberts, 'Did you ever notice how red Mary Jessup's hands are? They are ugly looking. I am glad that my hands don't look that way. I think I have beautiful hands.'

" ' Well, well,' answered her teacher, 'I

Almira Harrison leaves the log cabin for school, carrying her *McGuffy Reader*, slate and lunch.

think Mary Jessup has beautiful hands. Do you know, Daisy, Mary's hands are beautiful because of all of the nice and kind things she does. Mary's hands wash the dishes; they help her mother wash the clothes; they clean and sweep the floor. Sometimes when her mother is baking, Mary assists her in making cookies, cakes and pies. When her baby sister cries, Mary holds her and sings songs. She even goes next door and helps her neighbor lady. If her little girl is being naughty because she is having her hair washed, Mary tells her stories, which help her to be good. In fact, Mary is always looking for ways she can be helpful to those around her.'

" 'Oh, Miss Roberts,' said Daisy, 'I see what you mean. I know my hands need to do nice things like Mary does. From now on I shall do my best to make my hands really beautiful.' After this Daisy tried to do nice things, too."

When Almira brought her McGuffey reader books home, she read stories to both her father and mother. One evening after she had finished several stories, Judge Harrison said to Mrs. Harrison, "You know, Mother, I am so very glad the parents decided to go together and purchase these books.

"They are certainly character building, they teach our children to have good morals, good manners, to be honest, to treat their parents with respect, to share and to love God and those about them."

The original *McGuffy's First Reader* contained illustrations like this to accompany the moralistic readings.

CHAPTER 57 - MC GUFFEY'S READERS

The author of this book, *The Life of Judge Bazel Harrison*, found an article in the *Kalamazoo Gazette* dated September 25, 1976. This article gives us an excellent description of the author and of the *McGuffey Readers*.

McGuffey's Readers Molded The Minds Of Many In the 1800's

"It has been estimated that the minds and morals of 100 million Americans of the 19th Century were molded by *McGuffey School Readers*.

"Exactly 140 years ago, William McGuffey and his publishers contracted to produce the first of his noted books that were designed to teach pioneers the first and most important of the 'Three R's.'

"The first of the series of little school books appeared in Cincinnati. In the generations that followed, *McGuffey's Readers* were classified as best sellers.

"The books brought lasting fame to the author. There is a special shrine in his honor at Greenfield Village Museum in Dearborn.

"*McGuffey's Ecletic Readers* made their debut in 1836 in little red schoolhouses around the Midwest. They were packed with nuggets of knowledge.

"The books presented classical gems, re-written proverbs, adapted fables, folklore, myths,

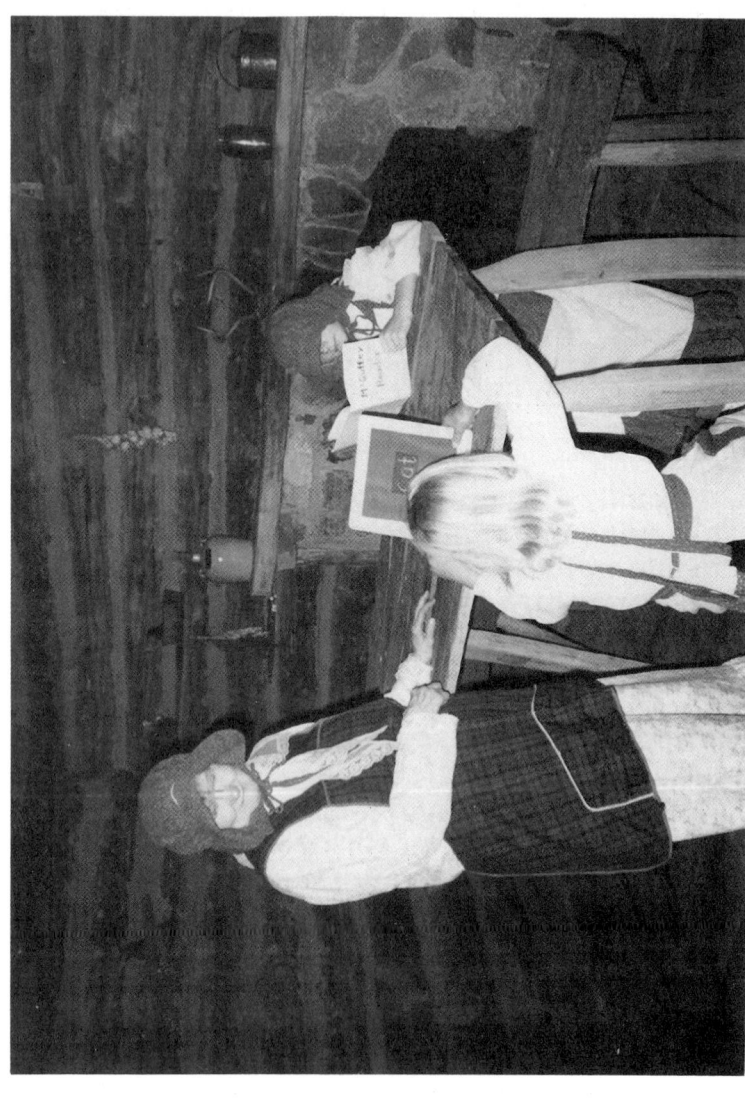

Eleven-year-old Almira Harrison is reading her *McGuffy Reader* while her niece studies her spelling words with her slate.

psalms, the cream of oratory and drama. The Miami University of Ohio professor also sprinkled in fiction and history, along with the utterances of sages, statesmen and poets.

"All these ingredients were blended with the proper proportions of adventure, love, humor and pathos. There was hardly a lesson in any of the books which failed to emphasize some moralistic message about patriotism, honesty, politeness, courage or truthfulness.

"From these volumes, frontier children and later their children learned that virtue always triumphed, that sin and evil were inevitably punished.

"There was for instance the tale of Frank Brown. On his way to school, Frank met a bad boy who tempted him to go down to the pond. Poor Frank fell in and drowned. The moral of the story is don't play with bad boys and don't stop to play on your way to school.

"Truthfulness came out in the story of George Washington, his ax and the cherry tree. Patience was the lesson in the story about the hare and the tortoise. 'Plain, plodding people, we often shall find, will leave hasty, confident people behind.'

"Other episodes warned against the depravity of robbing birds' nests, breaking girls' dolls, becoming dunces and sampling the grape. Quoth McGuffey -- 'No little boy or girl should drink rum or whisky or wine unless they want to become drunkards.'

"The last edition of the readers was issued in 1920 and, within the next two decades, they almost disappeared from the schools. Then began a remarkable revival of interest in them.

"Moved by sentiment, men and women who had grown up with the readers began to form McGuffey societies and hold reunions. The movement was similar to what the Trekkies have been doing because of their allegiance to the defunct Television series Star Trek. One of the McGuffey enthusiasts was Henry Ford. The Detroit automaker was a collector of McGuffey memorabilia."

The McGuffy Readers, which were used in Michigan schools.

CHAPTER 58 - CHIEF SAGAMAW

When the pioneers came to Michigan, they found the state to be in the possession of the Indians. In the vicinity of Kalamazoo County, the Potawatomies were their neighbors. Since these Indians travelled from place to place, they lived in wigwams.

We will concentrate our thoughts on about 250 Indians who lived on a reservation west of the town of Schoolcraft. According to residents who lived neighbor to them, they were friendly, kind and pursued peaceful lives. Sometimes they fought other tribes, but they never harassed their white newcomers.

These Indians lived on corn they had planted; on wild animals, which were in abundance, blueberries, blackberries and other fruits which grew wild. They also had gardens and dried vegetables for winter consumption.

They carried on a lively trade with the settlers, offering cranberries, maple sugar, deerskins, moccasins and wild fruits in exchange for flour, salt, tobacco, lead and, of course, whisky. The latter was of poor quality, consisting of the real stuff, watered down.

Let us now go to the reservation. Here the Indian Chief Sagamaw lived. He was the leader of his local tribe. He was such an outstanding person that he deserves to receive honorable mention of the highest sort.

Some of the Indians were not very consid-

Epaphroditus Ransom

As the Indians passed the home of Judge
Epaphroditus Ransom on their way west, they waved
their hands in a token of respect.

erate of their squaws, but we will find him to be thoughtful and a loving, kind husband.

The following story is told by one of the residents of the town of Schoolcraft:

"As I was riding my horse along the main downtown street, suddenly I heard the clop clop of a horse's hoofs. I realized that riding on the pony was Chief Sagamaw and his Indian squaw. I brought my horse to a halt and let their pony go by. As I watched this couple reach Mr. Houston's Store, I noticed the Chief said the Indian word 'Whoa'. The pony stopped. The Chief dismounted, held out his hand and grasped that of Mrs. Sagamaw. He then took her arm and gently helped her down from the pony. I was amazed at the courtesy he showed her. I thought I would ride my horse up and down the block.

Sagamaw had tied his pony to a hitching post. After a few minutes, they emerged from the store. I wondered what he would do now. So, I watched. When they came to their pony, the Chief placed his hand on the ground, she placed one foot in it and he lifted her with apparent ease on to the back of the pony."

Sagamaw was known for his oratory. Even though the settlers could not understand his words, his people did and they would listen to him with utmost attention. He was a man of integrity and had a dignified air about him. He always paid his bills and never owed anyone.

Perhaps you remember when Mr. Harrison

first arrived in Prairie Ronde how Chief Sagamaw led him and some of his companions to a body of water which was later named Harrison Lake. Then how the Chief and his 11 braves were of a great help in aiding Mr. Harrison build his log cabin.

Often when the Harrison family went to their door, they would find food that had been left by these kind friends.

These Indians were happily living on the land which had belonged to their ancestors for centuries. However, as more and more settlers began to arrive, they began to seize this land without paying for it. In spite of this, the Indians remained friendly and did not retaliate. Treaties were made, but our dear friends lost five million acres of land in lower Michigan. In exchange, they were given military trappings, baubles and trinkets for which they had little use. A wonderful friendship had sprung up between the residents of Michigan and the Potawatomies, but this association would soon be severed. For, in 1840 government officials decided they would force these people to leave the land which had belonged to their ancestors for hundreds of years.

They were commanded to rendezvous at a location just west of where the Amtrak Train Station now stands in Kalamazoo.

Fortunately, Chief Sagamaw did not have to face the indignity nor the humiliation which this command would bring because he was shot

An Indian Reservation located about two miles west of Schoolcraft where Chief Sagamaw lived with his people. Chief Sagamaw and other Indians were buried at this site.

and killed before the order was received.

In his book *Kalamazoo and How It Grew*, Willis Dunbar stated that "The Indians were encamped for several days before the day they were to start their trek west. They visited with local residents, many of whom had developed a warm and real friendship for individual Indians. From the north and the west, they assembled for the march beyond the Mississippi. The tents and household goods were loaded on the backs of the ponies. The sick and the aged also were carried on their backs. Men, women and children, accompanied by dogs, followed on foot. Papooses were carried on the backs of the squaws. They were apprehensive of the danger from the Sioux Tribe in the area assigned to them. But, they had no recourse.

"We may picture them as they started slowly on their trek to the West, a long line of sad and lonely people. Along the route they passed the home of Judge Epaphroditus Ransom, a prominent Kalamazoo man who often had befriended them in their dealings with the government. As they passed by, they all raised their hands in a last token of respect and farewell."

CHAPTER 59 - BAZEL HARRISON, KALAMAZOO'S FIRST JUDGE

"I tell you! You did it."

"It is your fault, not mine."

"You neglected to keep your wagon in repair."

"No," said one angry voice.

"Yes, but you broke the axle on my wagon and if you don't fix it than I shall sue you for all you have."

These were the voices of two Prairie Ronde settlers who were arguing about who should pay for a broken axle on a wagon owned by John Marcus.

Christopher Bair had borrowed a wagon which belonged to John Marcus and during the time he had used it the axle broke. Now the question was who should pay for it to be fixed. These two men came to Judge Bazel Harrison's home to have the dispute settled. Why did they come to Bazel Harrison and not to someone else?

The answer was simple. You see, by 1829 more settlers were arriving and the community was growing. There must be some organization of government affairs.

On December 14, 1830 a township meeting was held. At this election an attempt was made to organize. Mr. Harrison was chosen as justice of the peace and was commissioned by Governor Cass to be one of the judges of the county

First Co. Court held at the City of Kalamazoo, in a Log Cabin, Oct., 1832: In the rear are seated the Judges, Titus Bronson, Bazel Harrison and Stephen Hoyt. In front of the Judges' bench at a rude table, the Clerk, Stephen Vickery, is keeping the record. Sheriff, H. B. Houston. Attorneys: John Hascall, Cyrus Lovell and L. I. Daniels. Jury, James Smith, Jr., A. I. Shafer, John Brown, Jesse Abby, A. Cooley, Resen Holmes, Ebenezer Walter, Simeon Mills, Erastus Smith, and others. Parties to first suit, Robert Frakes vs. Isaac Brown.

Anthony Cooey painted this scene from memory in 1857.

- 220 -

court. He acted in this capacity until 1834. This is why the two arguing men came to Judge Harrison to have their grievance settled. And was the problem solved? It certainly was and in a very quick and diplomatic way. When they presented their problem, Judge Harrison knew he had an answer. He invited the men to enter his log cabin and asked Mrs. Harrison to slice off pieces of corn meal mush and fry them. Of course, the men were delighted and soon forgot the argument, so busy were they enjoying that delicious breakfast topped with maple syrup.

While they were eating, what did the judge do? He went to a box he had brought from Ohio and found just the right part. The axle was repaired and the men left with great rejoicing.

CHAPTER 60 - PLANNING A HOUSE RAISING

The Harrisons had been living in their log cabin for several years. It had done them great service and they enjoyed it very much. But, they had many, many obstacles regarding it because it was so small. However, Mr. and Mrs. Harrison were always able to take care of everybody that came to visit them. It was amazing what they were able to do with the 18 by 20 foot cabin. But, they had a loft made, which did help in the matter of sleeping.

One day Judge Harrison said to his wife, "Martha, it is time for us to think about a new house. We've had this log house a long time now and we should build a new frame house, one with boards, not with logs. Since the saw mill is operating now, we can bring the boards up here and I suggest that we have a house raising."

"Oh, Bazel," said Martha, "I think that would be wonderful! I would really love to have one. We can get started on the plans now. I enjoy things like that."

Judge Harrison said, "Yes, Martha, I have been to a number of them and through the years have helped other people build their log cabins and frame houses. I feel sure that it would be all right to invite our friends and neighbors to help. We should be able to get a few people to come. I don't know how many would respond to the invitation.

The famous Schoolcraft corn was once considered the best in the nation.

"If you feel this is what we should do, I will go to the Smith-Houston Store and put a notice about the event in the window. We could call it a house raising and corn fest and have it at the time the sweet corn is ripe.

"Let's ask the people who respond to bring kettles. Then we can have as many fires as we need. We will heat the water and put in the corn so it will be ready when it is time to eat. We can serve that freshly picked corn with sweet butter fresh from the churn."

"Oh, that a sounds so good," Martha replied. "You know, we have an unusually good crop this year."

"Yes," said the Judge. "I have noticed how tall the stalks are. I am tall, but these corn stalks are much higher than I am. They are just huge. This land is a gold mine. The rich, black soil makes everything grow so well. I am so thankful that we decided to settle in Prairie Ronde. You know, Martha, we have the cream of the crop. In a couple of weeks I think the corn will be ready and the boards for the house should be here by then."

Mr. Harrison printed the notice very carefully. It announced that there would be a house raising, a pot luck lunch and corn fest at his farm on August 31st and the Harrisons would provide all the corn anyone could eat. He left the notice in the store window, wondering how his neighbors might respond. He was most anxious to know what they might say to Mr.

Pictured is a stove similar to that which may have been used in the new frame house instead of a fireplace. Butter was made in the churn not unlike the one shown at the DeLano Homestead.

Smith and Mr. Houston and was sure that the store owners would tell him how the residents of Prairie Ronde felt about the invitation.

The Harrisons began their plans. "You know, Dad," said Martha, "we will have to plan a drink. At most of the house raisings, the host serves alcoholic beverages. The guests really do expect it, but we cannot let down our standards now. I don't think we have ever had such a drink in this cabin in all the years we have been here."

"That's right, Martha, we will continue to hold our standards high," said the Judge, "even if no one comes when they realize that the Harrisons allow no drinking on their premises. We know how injurious the 'fire water', as the Indians call it, is. We can serve tea, coffee, milk and sweet cider."

It has been told that Judge Harrison never drank anything but milk and this may be one reason for his excellent health and the fact that he lived to be 103 years old without being sick a day in his life.

After the sign had been in the store a few days, Judge Harrison thought he would make some purchases and check on the reactions of the customers. When he entered the store, Mr. Smith and Mr. Houston were delighted to see him again.

"Oh, Judge," Mr. Smith exclaimed, "since you put that sign in the window, we have had a lot of responses about you and your invitation.

"Everyone who read the sign seems to be very receptive. It looks as if you will have a huge crowd. Not only are they willing to help with the house raising, but we have heard some very complimentary things said about you.

"You know, Judge, we didn't know just how popular you are and we are learning from the people that you have special characteristics that make you an outstanding person, not only the wisdom you show in handling court cases, but we've heard a lot of things that let us know how very special you are. We would be glad to share some of their ideas with you. We think it would encourage you."

"Yes," said the Judge, "that would be very nice. I would like to know how our neighbors view us."

"Some of the things we have heard," continued Mr. Smith, "regard the way you and Mrs. Harrison open your log cabin to travelers, ministers, missionaries and anyone who needs a place to stay overnight or even for a few days. They say your home is like a hotel; that you always have an abundance of food for the hungry and you never turn anyone away.

"Those travelers who have stayed overnight go away encouraged and blessed by your kind hospitality. They not only have their physical needs supplied, but their spiritual needs as well. They enjoy the Bible reading you have each morning and evening. And, they tell us, that your personality just bubbles over. Your smiles and outgoing spirit have been referred to as a benediction."

Mr. Harrison was humbled by this report. He responded, "This is really something. I never realized that anyone felt this way about me. If they are saying such nice things, I had better be careful and not get the big head. Of course, it is important to me and to my family to follow God's teaching in our lives. I know Martha will be happy to hear what you said.

"You and your families are invited to our house raising and corn fest also. We don't expect you to work, but please join us after you close the store."

CHAPTER 61 - THE HOUSE RAISING

Mr. Harrison had engaged one of the settlers who had a special skill. It was that of organizing and putting a house together. He had experience in going to such affairs and he knew how to get a group of men together in such a way that they could accomplish a great deal in a short time.

Mrs. Harrison said to her husband, "I don't think we should pick the corn until everyone arrives. In this way we can plan to have just the right amount. You know that sweet corn is at its best when freshly picked."

"I guess you are right, Martha. I have found this to be true. I hope we will have enough workers to accomplish the feat in one day. Of course, if they don't finish, I think some of the men will come back until the task is done." The Harrisons were putting on the final touches to the arrangements.

At last the day arrived! It was a beautiful August morning, not too hot and not too cold. They could not have asked for a better day. Mrs. Harrison had suggested to Almira that she be responsible for taking care of the little children who would come with their families. She could organize games and races and be the Children's Activity Director. Almira thought this would be great fun. Having grown up in a big family, she knew how to keep children busy.

John and Bazel, Jr. would find things for

the older children to do until the time came to pick the sweet corn, when one of the men would join them in the field and reach the corn that was out of reach for the boys. Husking and cooking the corn took quite a bit of time and it was nearly two o'clock when dinner was served. This was to be the big meal of the day and in the evening, those who remained would feast on leftovers.

The Harrisons were used to having big picnics in the yard and had tables made of split logs which were fastened together. They were made with the smooth side up and they were now heaped with good food which the "house raisers" contributed. When all the guests gathered together to eat, they were amazed to see how many people had come.

Bazel Junior and John had taken care of the horses when the workers arrived, putting them out to pasture where they could stand in the shade of the trees and graze on the green grass.

It was understood by most of their pioneer friends that the Harrisons always had a blessing before they ate. Many of them had been in the Harrison home for meals and were used to this habit. Once everyone had found a place to sit, it was whispered Mr. Harrison would say the blessing. The men, women and even the very little children became very quiet, and bowed their heads. Mr. Harrison was pleased to see them so reverent.

He began, "Dear Heavenly Father, we are gathered together today in this manner to not only enjoy this food which you have so graciously provided, but to thank you for the way you have brought us through the trials of being pioneers. Martha and I thank you for sending such a large number here today to put up this house. We thank you for the sacrifice they are making for us. We ask you to bless this food to the strengthening of our bodies. May our fellowship be sweet and may we feel thy presence. We also thank you for this beautiful day. We ask all this in thy Name. Amen."

The sweet corn was ready and the aroma was tantalizing. Some of the men had brought tongs to retrieve the dripping ears and put huge platters of corn on the tables. And, of course, the food brought by those pioneers was delicious. Everyone ate their fill and there was still enough for the evening meal.

The house was going up so quickly that the main part of it would be completed by the time everyone went home. Some of the men promised to come back to help with some of the finishing work.

When everyone felt it was time to quit for the day, they sat on the ground just talking. Someone said, "Let's hold hands and sing some hymns." Of course, the Harrison family was well acquainted with many of the hymns that had been written by that time, having learned them before they moved from Ohio. Mr. Harrison's tenor voice rang out loud and clear as he led them in "Oh, Worship the King", "Love Divine" and a number of other favorites.

Soon it was time to go, but everyone shook hands and agreed that this was truly a sacred day that would be long remembered.

The log cabin was used as a tool shed, until it burned down.

(Author's postscript)

As a final statement, I would like to say the sweet corn which was so much enjoyed that day is still being grown in Prairie Ronde. At one time, a local farmer who entered a national contest, won a prize for growing the best corn in the United States. An article in the Kalamazoo Gazette had a story regarding this news. If you go to Schoolcraft in August and early September, you will be able to confirm what I am saying.

When Governor Cass commissioned Bazel Harrison to be judge of Kalamazoo County, he had just completed his new frame house. It was right after the house raising and the potluck.

CHAPTER 62 - OAK OPENINGS OR
THE BEE HUNTER

This story took place in the downtown section of Schoolcraft on July 8, 1848. It was a warm Saturday night. The main street which ran through this little town was crowded with shoppers. Farmers and residents had assembled in front of the open stores. The ladies and little girls were wearing their long calico dresses. The boys were dressed in knee length trousers.

Let us listen to the sounds coming from the noisy, buzzing throng as the latest news is discussed. Wagons are clattering along the unpaved road as the drivers are trying to find parking spots. Buggies, some with tops up and some with tops down, were trying to squeeze into available spaces that were left. Horses whose drivers were fortunate enough to arrive first and had parking spaces, were whinnying and stamping their feet. They were patiently waiting for their masters or mistresses to emerge from the crowds to untie them from the hitching posts. What a buzzing sound the crowd is making, standing in front of the stores.

Let us walk down on the outer edge of the gathering to see if we can find anyone we know. We are rewarded as we come upon Abner Cox and Ronald Randall who were busily discussing some weighty subject. Curious to know what this subject was, I asked if they cared if we joined them. Abner Cox said, "We would be de-

James Fenimore Cooper may have looked out of this window after a day of searching for information which he could use in writing *Oak Openings*.

lighted to have you meet with us."

As we came closer to them, Abner Cox said to his friend, "You know, Ronald Randall, I was just asking where you have been. I have missed you lately."

"Well, well," answered Ronald, "I have been to Kalamazoo looking for work, but since I could not find any, I returned to Schoolcraft. Perhaps I can find a farmer around here who would like an extra hand."

"While you were in Kalamazoo, did you hear any news we in Schoolcraft should be aware of?"

"Yes, I did," answered Ronald, "and I have it first hand. Do you remember James Fenimore Cooper who stayed with Judge Hezekiah Wells several years ago? I believe he was hiking to places around here gathering information for a book he was planning to write. I think he called it *Oak Openings*. I believe he said that he visited the Big Island Forest, which he said was a perfect setting for his book."

"No, I don't remember him," answered Abner Cox.

"Now I learned," continued Ronald, "that he has finished his book and it will soon be released. I believe there will be an article in the *Kalamazoo Gazette* about it which will be delivered here next Friday."

(The *Gazette*, which started in 1833 was formerly called *The Statesman* and was published in White Pigeon. After the Land Office was moved to Kalamazoo, *The Statesman* became the *Gazette*).

"I heard the *Gazette* is planning to include a short biography of Mr. Cooper in this edition. I think we should tell everyone we know about this coming news. I shall start to advertise this Friday's edition tonight while the crowd is still here."

The word spread like wildfire because on the following Friday when the wagon that delivered the weekly mail from Kalamazoo to Schoolcraft arrived at the Post Office, crowds of people were on hand. The store keepers were there as well as the *Gazette's* weekly customers. Fortunately, there were extra papers included in the delivery.

Farmers and town residents bought the extra papers from the stores and soon could be seen standing around reading the contents.

CHAPTER 63 - A BIOGRAPHY OF JAMES FENIMORE COOPER

Since there were not enough papers to go around because the demand was so great, Mr. Randall told the disappointed residents to gather around him and he would read his paper to them.

He began to read. Some looked over his shoulder at the front page. There at the top, in large letters were the words: "COOPER'S NOVEL, *OAK OPENINGS*, TO BE RELEASED SOON." In small letters were these words, "see page 2 for his biography." Ronald read aloud to the eager group.

"James Fenimore Cooper was born in 1790 in Burlington, New Jersey. When he was a year old his parents moved to the State of New York where they bought a great deal of land. Mr. Cooper resold this land and became very wealthy. The town of Cooperstown was named for him. Little James grew up surrounded by wealth and luxury. He received anything and everything he wanted.

"At the age of 13 he entered Yale University. He was the youngest boy in his class as well as being the best Latin student. Perhaps he was the youngest student who entered Yale up to this time. In his Junior year he played a prank on one of the tutors and for this was dismissed. A few years later he joined the Navy, but this career lasted only a few years as he be-

became interested in becoming an author.

"Up to this time the books which were published came from Europe. American authors had not started to write.

"It so happened that James Fenimore Cooper felt the urge to write novels regarding the American way of living. He was a contemporary of the famous Washington Irving.

"He decided to study frontier and Indian life and use these ideas as a background for his novels.

"His first novel, *Precaution,* which was published in 1821, was a failure. In spite of this experience, he continued to write. He wrote and published the following books: *The Pioneers* in 1823; *The Last of the Mohicans,* 1826; *The Prairie,* 1827; *The Path Finder,* 1840; and *The Deerslayer,* 1841. These five books were known as *The Leatherstocking Tales.*

"He achieved great success and he soon was heralded as a national and international author. He ranked with Washington Irving in his fame.

"In the early 1840's, he heard about Michigan, Kalamazoo and its river, Schoolcraft and Prairie Ronde. He understood this section of the United States was becoming famous for its opportunities for settlement. By this time, because of the royalties from his successful books and his father's wealth, he became a country gentleman who could be a man of leisure. However, the lure of owning more land led him to go to Michigan where he wished to invest in its opportunities. He also desired to continue gathering information for another book, which he planned to write.

"So, in the early 1840's he started to make trips to Michigan with Prairie Ronde and Kalamazoo as his destination. At this time he could come by the Erie Canal via Buffalo and Detroit. He could then either come by stage coach, rent a buggy or covered wagon. These vehicles would travel the Territorial Road to Kalamazoo. Here his nephew, Horace Comstock, could pick him up if he came by stage coach. He then would stay with his niece and nephew while he explored the countryside gathering information. So, during the years of 1840 to 1850, this is what he did in connection with his land investments.

"In the next edition of the *Gazette*, there will be a short biography of Horace Comstock, who married Cooper's niece."

An account of this biography will be the subject of the next chapter.

On the following Friday, the same events, which had taken place the previous week were repeated.

Horace Comstock built the first frame house in the community named after him. There the Literary Society named Bazel Harrison as the role model for Cooper's Bee Hunter

CHAPTER 64 - A MINI-BIOGRAPHY OF HORACE COMSTOCK

On the front page of the Friday's edition of the *Gazette* appeared in large capital letters, "GENERAL HORACE COMSTOCK, A Mini-Biography...see page 2".

"General Horace Comstock was a native of Cooperstown, New York. This was true of his wife also. Since she was a niece of Mr. Cooper, perhaps they both lived near the Cooper family in New York. Comstock was a politician and a general. According to ADP VanBuren's writings for the Pioneer Collection, Volume 5, General Comstock was a courteous gentleman which made him popular; he was a lawyer, which gave him standing; he was a politician, which gave him influence; he was considered wealthy, which raised him still higher; but he took the highest rank of all for being the husband of a lovely lady of refinement. His kindness and generosity to the early settlers was proverbial.

"He and his refined, cultured wife had moved to Detroit about 1830. They were nicely settled when Mr. Comstock heard about Bronson and the possibilities of investing in land. So, he decided to leave his home and journey to this small town. He perhaps rented a covered wagon or buggy to make the trip. He would travel down the Territorial Road, which connected Detroit with St. Joseph, but also branched off and ended at Bronson. If he came

Around 1850 Anthony Cooley painted Kalamazoo as he remembered it in 1832 (courtesy Kalamazoo Public Museum.)

by buggy, he could stay at inns along the way.

"When he neared Bronson, he stopped at a little hamlet which consisted of a few log cabins. They housed some of the early pioneers who had also come by way of the Erie Canal.

"As he arrived at this little settlement, which was to later bear his name, he was overwhelmed by its beauty. He was especially impressed by the Kalamazoo River as it meandered through the small village. He decided not to continue on to Bronson, but to remain in this location. He returned to Detroit to tell his wife his plans. He would build a beautiful frame house, the first of its kind. He followed through with his plans, and as a saw mill was established nearby, his construction workers had access to the sawed boards which were used in the building.

"In 1831 the house known as Comstock Manor and later, Brookside, was completed. It was very beautiful. It towered above the small log cabins. It was built on the bank of the Kalamazoo River, which presented a beautiful view.

"He returned to Detroit and brought his beautiful, kind and unassuming wife. She wished to make the log cabin dwellers happy. Instead of looking down on them due to her wealth, she neighbored with them and invited them to her home. Mr. Comstock was a very generous man and, if any of the settlers were in need of anything, he was eager to fill that need.

He gave away a considerable portion of his fortune and never expected the people to repay him. The inhabitants of this small village were so grateful for these favors, they decided to name it Comstock, in honor of him.

"He wished for the village to become the county seat, but he was disappointed in this wish. He introduced many improvements, such as building a free school and tried to make the Kalamazoo River navigable to its mouth. Some of these endeavors were too costly and unrealistic. However, his generosity and friendliness were long remembered."

In the next chapter, we will push ahead to the year 1846 to see how this charitable and outstanding couple played a great role in the life of their uncle, James Fenimore Cooper, in his writing of the book, *Oak Openings.*

James Fenimore Cooper, published *Oak Openings...* in 1848.

CHAPTER 65 - THE LITERARY
SOCIETY TAKES ACTION

We will leave the year 1848 and the publication of the book *Oak Openings* to go back to the year 1846, when Mr. Cooper had begun his novel. He decided this year to come to Kalamazoo, Prairie Ronde and Schoolcraft to gather more information. While he was in this vicinity, he would look after his real estate business.

Since a train had just started a run from Detroit to Kalamazoo, he would come by the way of the Erie Canal and board a train for the last lap of his journey. He had informed his nephew and niece of his intentions. Consequently, he expected Mr. Comstock to meet him at the station. When Mr. Cooper was nicely settled in the shiny, black buggy, he said, "Horace, you know that I am writing another book. The setting will be the Kalamazoo River, Kalamazoo, Schoolcraft and Prairie Ronde.

"The time will go back to when the Indians were here and before the first white settlers came. It will have as its hero, Ben Boden, who will be a bee hunter by vocation. Now, I am interested in finding a prototype or role model to use as a pattern for my hero. My parents, your great uncle and aunt, brought me up in such a way as to implant in me the right way of living. I have high ideals, you know, and I have always strived to be a man of high morals.

"In my story, I want to create a hero who has the same goals and even greater ones than I have. I would like to find a person around this area who would fulfill these requirements or fit this pattern."

When the two men arrived at Comstock Manor, Mr. Comstock said to his wife, "Dear, Uncle James is planning to write another book." He told her of their plans. This capable wife said, "Let's have a luncheon and invite the members of our Literary Society to come. Perhaps they will know of a person who has just the characteristics he wants his Ben Boden to have."

Arrangements were made and, as it was summer, they planned to have the discussion outdoors. The Literary Society members became very excited about the project.

"Let's invite the two reporters who write for the *Gazette* and *Telegraph*. I think they will want to cover these events," suggested Mr. Comstock.

The day came for this party to take place. The two reporters came early. One was James Stone, who wrote a "Biographical Sketch of Judge Bazel Harrison" in 1874. They stood by a window which overlooked the yard and drive. From now on our account of this gala event, in addition to what happened afterward, will appear as if written by Mr. Stone in the year 1846.

"The guests arrived in shiny, new wagons. They were the intelligentsia, the well-read, and the wealthy citizens of Kalamazoo and Prairie Ronde. The ladies were dressed in the latest fashion. Their long dresses were not of calico, but were of silks and satins.

"Most of the members of the Literary Society were from the East. They were acquainted with the famous books of European authors. They had also read the works of Poe, Emerson and Holmes. Of course, they had read Cooper's well-known novels as well as the writings of Washington Irving.

"The men were wearing stove pipe hats and were dressed in expensive black suits. As the ladies stepped down from the elegant wagons, they were escorted to the Manor by their husbands and were greeted by the gracious and charming Mrs. Comstock. Eliza, the cook, and Betsy, the maid, were putting the finishing touches on the preparations for the luncheon.

"After the meal was finished, everyone filed into the beautiful rose garden. Here they were going to carry on their discussion."

An 1891 edition of *Oak Openings* depicts Ben Boden hiding from the Indians in the wild rice at the mouth of the Kalamazoo River.

CHAPTER 66 - THE ROLE MODEL

"When everyone was seated, Mr. Comstock arose from his chair, 'Friends and members of the Literary Society, we are gathered together today in order to assist my Uncle James Fenimore Cooper, who has come from Cooperstown, New York and is writing his latest novel, *Oak Openings*.

"'I believe, since we are acquainted with many of the residents of Kalamazoo and Prairie Ronde, we would be capable of suggesting a prototype or role model for this hero, Ben Boden. I will now turn the meeting over to you, Uncle James.'

"Mr. Cooper stood and addressed the members of this elite society. He began his presentation with 'I thank all of you for coming today. I will get to my point immediately. I am very particular about the characteristics belonging to the person you are going to suggest as a role model for my hero, Ben Boden. You see, I am a person of high ideals, high morals and I lean toward a life that is beyond reproach.

"'Of course, I would want my Ben Boden to be all of this and more. I see Mrs. Daniels, who is a very favorite friend of long standing, is here. I believe she came to this vicinity many years ago and would be very capable in taking over the chairmanship of this meeting. I will now turn the discussion over to her.'

"Mrs. Daniels stood and said, 'I count it a

great honor, Mr. Cooper, for you to ask me to lead this discussion. Before we start on our suggestions, I feel, in order to simplify matters, I would like to put forth my input regarding the matter we have at hand. I have known Judge Bazel Harrison ever since I was a little girl. We arrived in Kalamazoo in 1834. Mr. and Mrs. Harrison were great friends of my father and mother and we traveled many times to Harrison Lake to visit them.

" 'If ever there was a man who would fulfill all of Mr. Cooper's requirements, I believe he is the one. Some of you know about the history of his life, but probably some of you do not. I shall take a few moments to review this and bring you up to date. In the year 1828 he, some of his family and neighbors left the comfort of civilization to journey to Michigan. They left an area near Cincinnati. There were 21 people in all, who courageously fought hardships of chopping down trees in order that their covered wagons and Conestoga could make a road for them to go through. They also brought 50 sheep and 50 hogs, 11 horses, three cows and two oxen.

" 'When they arrived at Harrison Lake, they built a log cabin with the help of the kind Indians. Mr. Harrison became the first judge of Kalamazoo County. He became famous for his wisdom in handling court cases regarding both the Indians and the other residents of this area.

" 'No one was ever turned away from his

humble home, but found lodging and food. Not only did they receive material blessings, but they received encouragement as well.

    " 'Mr. Harrison and Mrs. Harrison were highly respected and he became a leader in the community. I believe I have said enough along this line and we will spend the remainder of the afternoon visiting informally with Mr. Cooper. Those of you who know Mr. Harrison could inform him of your experiences. I believe that Ben Boden will be a bee hunter by vocation. Is this correct, Mr. Cooper? Now, I believe Mr. Harrison has been an inveterate one.' "

CHAPTER 67 - WAS HE COOPER'S BEE HUNTER? WE THINK HE WAS THE ORIGINAL BEN BODEN

The guests stayed all afternoon discussing the reasons for the decision they made. They had decided that Judge Bazel Harrison would be the one who should qualify for the honor of being the original Ben Boden. Let us turn to Mr. James Stone and his Biographical Sketch of Judge Bazel Harrison, which he wrote in 1874, to see what he says.

"It has been a matter of general belief for many years that Judge Harrison was the Bee Hunter of Cooper's novel, the Oak Openings, the scene of which, it will be remembered, is laid in Kalamazoo. Since the publication of the work, this has been the accepted theory among the pioneers of the county and Judge Harrison's neighbors. We never heard the fact questioned until last year, when Judge H. G. Wells informed us that Mr. Cooper told him after the appearance of the book, that his character of Ben Boden, the Bee Hunter, was not founded on Judge Harrison but on Towner Savage, one of the pioneers of the county, and a bee hunter by avocation. This being so, Mr. Cooper must have made contradictory statements, for Mrs. J. B. Daniels, of this village, is very positive and clear in her recollection that Mr. Cooper repeatedly named Judge Harrison as the original character mentioned.

"As we have said before, Mr. Cooper had considerable property interest in Kalamazoo County and the township north of it derived its name from him.

"Mrs. Daniels was well prepared to give such information as Mr. Cooper sought, and he afterwards acknowledged her services in this respect, by presenting her with a copy of *Oak Openings*, and at that time he told her that Judge Harrison was the original of the Bee Hunter. Mrs. Daniels also informs us that in frequent conversations with the old judge, he has stated to her that he understood that he was the person Cooper had in mind when he created Buzzing Ben and also that he had been so informed by Cooper himself. Last year we ourselves questioned Judge Harrison on this point, but his mind was not clear enough that day to comprehend the question. We have made a great deal of research to fix the identity of the Bee Hunter beyond question, and have talked with scores of old settlers. While we have found but few who claimed to have any direct information on the subject, all of the testimony except that of Judge Wells has been to confirm the theory that Bazel Harrison was the original of Mr. Cooper's character. Dozens of well known citizens have related to us an account of a conversation alleged to have taken place between Judge Harrison and Mr. Cooper, at the time of the novelist's last visit to Kalamazoo...the anecdote having been current since the incident is said to have occurred. Judge Harrison, so the story runs, having been introduced to Mr. Cooper, after the introduction remarked, 'So you got me into your book, Mr. Cooper?'

'Yes,' replied Mr. Cooper, 'I had to have someone Judge, and you seemed to be about the right sort of a person to make by bee hunter out of.'

We are forced to the conclusion, however, that Mr. Cooper must have had Judge Harrison in his mind when he drew the picture of Buzzing Ben the bee hunter, though, of course his por-traitor may have included the characteristics found in Towner Savage or other settlers."

Let us go directly to the actual book of *Oak Openings*, published by P. F. Collier in New York in 1892. On page 240 there is a description of an old gentleman. Could this be that of Bazel Harrison, Ben Boden's prototype?

"On one side of the island of wood lies the little village or the large hamlet of Schoolcraft. here we were most cordially welcomed by General Boden, and all of his descendants. The head of this family is approaching seventy, but is still hale and hearty. His head is as white as snow and his face as red as a cherry. A finer old man one seldom sees. Temperance, activity, the open air and a good conscience have left him a noble ruin, if ruin he can yet be called. He owes the last blessing, as he told us himself, to the fact that he kept clear of the whirlwind of speculation that passed over this region some ten or fifteen years since. His means are ample and the harvest being about to commence, he invited me to the field."

Could this period of speculation be the land boom in about the years of 1835 to 1840 when Kalamazoo and Schoolcraft enjoyed those prosperous years when settlers came from far and near to buy land?

A vignette from the 1873 edition of *Oak Openings.*

CHAPTER 68 - BAZEL HARRISON AND THE SCHOOLCRAFT UNITED METHODIST CHURCH...A HISTORY TO 1851

The following is an imaginary account of the part Bazel and Martha Harrison played in the beginning of this church.

The basic facts are true and were gleaned from a paper which was presented to the author by the Reverend Dwight Burson, who is the present pastor.

In was August 5th, 1832. Judge Harrison, after a hot day working in the fields, was relaxing under a shade tree in front of his log cabin.

Martha Harrison, Worlenda and daughter Martha were cooking supper over an open fire. During the summer they did everything they could out of doors in order that the cabin would stay cool.

A kettle of vegetables was suspended from a pole which was laid across the ends of two sticks that had been pounded into the ground. They were giving off a tantalizing aroma as they bounced around in the kettle. In a large frying pan resting on the hot coals fresh pork chops were sizzling in pork grease. The day before, Judge Harrison had butchered one of this hogs.

Mrs. Harrison and her daughters were taking turns turning the chops so they would become a golden brown.

On the split log table there was a pitcher

The First United Methodist Church of Schoolcraft evolved from services held in the Bazel Harrison barn. Martha and Bazel Harrison were charter members of this church.

of milk which had been kept cool in the root cellar. We will learn more about this in a future chapter. Of course, there was the customary Johnny cake lying in the middle of the table and beside it was a dish of fresh wild honey. Judge Harrison had found a new hive the day before.

All of a sudden, the sound of a horse's hoofs reached the ears of the family. Judge Harrison looked up in time to see a galloping horse coming up the driveway. The rider said, "whoa". The horse stopped and the man dismounted. He came over to the Judge who was standing with an outstretched hand. Smiling, Mr. Harrison said, "Welcome stranger, you look as if you have been riding a long way."

"I certainly have," he said. "Prince and I have been on the road since early morning. My name is Felton, James Felton and I am from the Ohio Methodist Conference. I am here to see if I can help the Prairie Ronde residents start a church."

"Oh! this is wonderful. We need a church, Reverend Felton," said the Judge.

"You see," said the newcomer, "I didn't know who I should interview regarding the proposition, so I stopped at the Smith Houston Store. Mr. Houston said to see you because you are a leader in the community and a very devout man. I believe you have devotions morning and evening, do you not?"

"We certainly do, Reverend Felton, and we also entertain strangers. You will plan to make your home with us while you carry out your plans, won't you?"

"Absolutely, Mr. Harrison, where else would I go?" questioned the minister.

Mr. Harrison called his family over to meet the minister. After the introductions, the Judge said to John and Bazel Junior, "Why don't you boys take Reverend Felton down to the lake for a swim so he can cool off? Supper will be ready in about half an hour."

The minister was delighted. He went to his saddle bags and took out some clean clothes. Twelve-year-old John spoke up and said, "Bazel, you go ahead and take our new friend down to the lake while I give his horse a rubdown and then take him to pasture."

Of course, Prince was very happy to receive the attention and whinnied to show his appreciation. Brownie made Prince feel right at home when he began to nuzzle him with his nose.

While eating the delicious meal, the Judge said, "We will do all we can to advertise a service, which I think you are planning for Sunday. Since this is Friday evening, I can spend most of Saturday after the chores are finished inviting people to the meeting.

Saturday dawned bright and clear. The evening before had cooled off so everyone slept well. After breakfast, Mr. Harrison found a spot under a shade tree where one could feel a cool breeze coming from Harrison Lake. He invited the pastor to spend the morning relaxing in a comfortable chair in order to prepare his Sunday sermon.

He then saddled Brownie, kissed his wife and children good-bye and started on his special mission. He knew he must find a place for the meeting. It would have to be large enough to hold a big crowd. He thought of a school which was located on the corner of 12th Street and U Avenue. He was pretty certain that his friend who lived on the Five Pines Farm would give permission for the Prairie Ronde residents to use it for the Sunday gathering. One reason for using this school was because it was centrally located.

He contacted the owner, Richard Homes, who was very happy when he heard about having a church service and heartily assented. Judge Harrison invited him to come too. "You can count on me," he said, "I have felt right along that we needed a service in which to worship the Lord."

"Good," said the Judge, "we will see you tomorrow."

Judge Harrison mounted Brownie. We will now jump on our horse and follow Brownie and the Judge as they travel to the Smith Houston Store, where he plans to place a conspicuous sign announcing the Sunday meeting.

Mr. Smith and Mr. Houston were thrilled with the idea and said they would certainly attend.

Sunday was another beautiful day, not too hot and not too cool. The Harrison family was able to walk the short distance to the schoolhouse. When they arrived there were many wagons and ox carts parked wherever they could find a place. The horses were neighing and making quite a noise. They acted as if they were happy, too, to be able to observe Sunday.

The ladies and girls were dressed up in their long calico dresses and their matching sun bonnets. Some of the men, who had come from the Eastern states by way of the Erie Canal, were wearing their black suits and stove pipe hats. However, Judge Harrison and the men who did not own expensive attire, were just as happy as those who did.

What a refreshing and spiritual time everyone had, singing the old hymns which had been composed before 1832. The congregation knew many of the songs as they had sung them in the churches they had attended before they had come "West" to Prairie Ronde.

At the close of the meeting, Reverend Felton gave an opportunity for those who had spiritual needs to remain after the service. He then said, "If there are any of you who would like to organize and become a nucleus of a church, please raise your hand."

Fifteen people responded. They would become charter members of the future Schoolcraft Methodist Church.

Those who accepted the challenge were the

The Rev. James T. Robe preached his first sermon in Schoolcraft the winter of 1832-33.

following: Nathan Cobb, Sally Cobb, Josiah Duncan, Polly Duncan, Mary Frakes, Louisa Cooper, Darius Wells, Mary Wells, Rebecca Brudner, Ruth Lloyd, and a local preacher the Reverend H.B.Cooke and his wife; Bazel Harrison, Martha Harrison and George Fletcher, who became a class leader for 40 years. He was also the great-grandfather of Mrs. Bessie Lukes, who became a member of the Methodist Church in 1957.

Since Reverend Felton as a circuit rider, would have to travel over a large territory serving a number of churches, he would be able to come to the Schoolcraft Church only once a month.

After he began his ministry in Michigan he had to return to Ohio because of poor health. He had not been home long when the Lord called him to his Heavenly reward.

The Indiana Conference heard about this dilemma and sent Reverend James Robe to continue this work. His territory embraced Little Prairie Ronde, LaGrange Prairie and the area north of the St. Joseph River.

Elder Robe found that he, too, could only come once a month. The entire parish was called the Kalamazoo Mission. He also started the Methodist Church in Bronson. He preached his first sermon at Prairie Ronde at the home of Darius Wells, which was the only place of meeting during the winter. In 1833, a quarterly meeting was held there. People came from far and near to attend. Some of them came in ox carts.

In August of the same year, a camp meeting was held on the Bishop Farm, where the first Sunday School was organized. Erastus Williams was the Superintendent. When summer came, Judge Harrison's barn was used for church services.

Another quarterly meeting was held April 6, 1833, at a school house about one mile north of Harrison Corners or Liberty Pole, as it was so often called. This meeting was held by the Reverend James Armstrong. Reverend Robe was succeeded by Reverend Richard Max and to the mission was added Bronson, now Kalamazoo. Reverend Max stayed two years and was succeeded by Reverend Thomas Erastus Kellogg, with H.B.Beers and Jacob Colater as assistants.

After 20 years, Reverend Robe returned to Schoolcraft from Indiana and continued for some time. The history of the new church began in 1851. The dedication took place on March 28, 1852. We will skip down to the present time. Much of this history, which is an account of the Methodist Church after Reverend Felton left Prairie Ronde, was copied from a paper which the author received from Reverend Burson.

CHAPTER 69 - EXCAVATIONS AT SITE OF HARRISON CABIN

The following stories are taken from three *Kalamazoo Gazette* articles and from a paper written by Mr. Alexis Praus, Curator of the local Museum and Mr. Paul Millikan, Professor of History at Kalamazoo Valley Community College.

The titles of the newspaper clippings are as follows: "The Search for Building Site of County's Earliest Settler," September 13, 1955; "They Dig That Digging, KVCC Students Taking an Archaeological Approach In Seeking Historic Cabin Site," by Victor Rauch, May 25, 1969; "KVCC's Dig-In Is Paying Off" by Victor Rauch, June 19, 1969.

The first part of the narration will take us to the Kalamazoo Public Library where we will meet two staff members, Mr. Alex Praus and Miss Lillian Anderson.

The year is 1956. Mr. Praus happened to come across an old county plat map. As he looked at it, he said to himself, "Well, well, this map shows Harrison Lake. I think I've heard about Judge Bazel Harrison, who was the first settler in Kalamazoo County. I wonder if this is the same man after whom the lake is named. I guess I will check it out in a history book."

He found an old one in the library which confirmed his thoughts. This book also said, "Judge Harrison was one of the best liked men in the county and never had an enemy. He died at age 103."

Mr. Praus left the room and started down the hall. As he did so, he met Miss Lillian Anderson, one of the librarians. "Oh! Lillian," he said, "do you know what? I just had an idea. Perhaps you know how I've dug up and collected relics from early Kalamazoo. I have discovered another project."

"What is it?" questioned Miss Anderson.

"You see, Lillian, I am a museum director, but I am at heart an archeologist. I just discovered a possible site to do some digging."

That sounds interesting," commented Miss Anderson. "Just what do you plan to do?"

"It's this way, Lillian. I would like to go to Harrison Lake. I guess you know where it is, just west of Schoolcraft."

"Yes," she said, "I do know something about the lake. I believe the first log cabin in this county was built near it."

"I would like to find some people who would go with me and perhaps we could dig up artifacts that belonged to the Harrison family. If we do, we could preserve them for the museum. We might find some remains from his cabin. However, I heard it was destroyed by fire sometime before 1900. I think I will go over to the Community College to visit my friend, Professor Paul Millikan. I believe he has done some digging in Virginia at Civil War battlefield sites. I will see what he has to say,"

"I wish you much success," responded Miss Anderson.

The next day, Mr. Praus did some planning. First he asked a friend, William G. West, a local radio and television dealer to come to his office. Mr. West had an Army land mine detector. Operating on the radar principle, this instrument was able to locate any density, such as would be in the ground at a spot where old cabin remains were buried.

A *Gazette* article, written September 9, 1955 said the following: "History records show approximately where the first Harrison cabin was built, but not exactly. A few years after coming to Kalamazoo County, the first cabin was abandoned and the family moved into a larger home."

The first try at digging for evidences of the cabin was in 1956. In order to understand the background of these excavations, let us leave the *Gazette* articles and transfer to an account of the diggings as written by Mr. Praus and Mr. Millikan for the museum.

Excavations revealed that the front door of Judge Bazil Harrison's cabin faced Harrison Lake, south of Schoolcraft.

ARCHAEOLOGICAL FINDINGS AT SITE OF HARRISON HOMESTEAD

By Paul Millikan

For some years the museum and historical associations of the Kalamazoo area have been interested in locating the exact site of the first settler's cabin built in Kalamazoo County, Michigan. Between May 12th and June 20th, 1969, a group of students from Kalamazoo Valley Community College, Kalamazoo, Michigan, entered upon an archaeological search for that site under the leadership and instruction of the authors.

Historical records identified the Harrison farm as the site of that first cabin built by Bazel Harrison in 1828. Local tradition pointed to an area of high ground at the east end of Harrison Lake, as the specific site of the cabin. With these leads, and those mentioned in the previous article, our group set out to prove or to disprove local tradition as to the location of the first permanent habitation in this county.

The search was carried out by scientific archaeological methods, and was done as a part of the college C.A.P. program. The initials C.A.P. stand for "College Approved Program", a three week period at the end of each semester designed to give the students a unique educational experience. Students may take a course in any subject area offered by the college during C.A.P.

John E. Crose, a great, great grandson of Bazel and Martha
Harrison.

sessions.

Bazel Harrison's funeral was on September 2, 1874 and at the home of his son, John S. Harrison, near the lake on which he settled in 1828. So many attended, probably 800 or so, that the service had to be held on the lawn of the house. One of those attending was a babe in his mother's arms who, in later years, helped to locate the site of Harrison's first log cabin.

In 1955 the Director of the Kalamazoo Public Museum and some volunteers tried to find the site of Bazel Harrison's pioneer log cabin. To find it would be to locate the exact place and the remains of Kalamazoo County's first permanent home. Evidences of habitation were found, but all were of a later date than the date of Harrison's advent to the prairie. However, at the close of the season, Mr. John Crose, the baby above, and now an elderly person, came to the writer's office and stated that he knew the location and would be happy to take him to it.

Subsequently, the site was pointed out by Mr. Crose who remembered the log cabin being used as a chicken coop, in the days of his youth. The account that follows tells of the successful archaeological exploration of Bazel Harrison's log cabin by students of the Kalamazoo Valley Community College on the shores of Lake Harrison in Prairie Ronde Township, Kalamazoo County.

NOTE: Information for part of this was taken from *A Biographical Sketch of Judge Bazel Harrison*, by James H. Stone,1874. Reprinted by *The Express*, Schoolcraft, Michigan. 1913. AAP

The location of artifacts and the first brick formation we uncovered indicated to us that the root cellar had been under the north end of the cabin. there was nothing to indicate a stairway in any of the walls, so the cellar must have been entered by a trap door in the cabin floor. We surmise that this cellar and the portion of the cabin over it must have been built sometime (probably one to five years) after the original cabin. The portion of the cabin built for the first winter certainly had a dirt floor. A wooden floor with a trap door to a root cellar would have been a luxury on the frontier, and would not have been built until after more essential construction on the farm had been completed.

Several other near-by squares were dug as well. At the end of our excavation we had several thousand artifacts: hundreds of square nails, thousands of pieces of glass and pottery, and many unidentifiable pieces. Several of the more important artifacts dated in the period from 1830 to 1870. Among the interesting items found were four pennies dated 1842, 184? and 1864; a flintlock from about 1830; the pendulum from a clock; a peppermint bottle; and bowls and stem fragments from clay pipes. These and several others are pictured here. All of the arti-

The 1842 coins were excavated by Kalamazoo Valley Community College students in 1969, along with many other Harrison artifacts which are presently housed in the Kalamazoo Public Museum in Kalamazoo, Michigan.

facts have been cataloged and are made a permanent part of the Kalamazoo Public Museum collection.

The conclusions of our dig were positive. We had established the exact location of Bazel Harrison's log cabin. We had determined the dimensions of the cabin and learned what building materials were used. We learned a great deal about the style of living of this first pioneer in the county, and reached many lesser conclusions as well.

This was a unique educational experience for community college students. Most college archaeology courses are offered only for upper classmen or even graduate students. Our students were highly motivated by their experience. They found this an exciting way to learn about the past. Their interest and enthusiasm was so great that they later formed an Archaeology Club, and even continued to pursue archaeology as a hobby. History came alive for them, perhaps for the first time. It became personal, too, and by the end of the project we all felt like Bazel Harrison was an old friend. Because the students were able to identify with the past, they felt a very rewarding fulfillment in what was accomplished in our project.

The project was also an enrichment experience for many students to whom history and archaeology had been considered dusty, somewhat boring studies, found only in books. The anticipation and challenge of searching for artifacts, finding them, researching them for identification and dates, then drawing conclusions, will not soon be forgotten.

ARTICLES FROM THE *KALAMAZOO GAZETTE*

KVCC's Dig-In Is Paying Off

by Victor Rauch, *Gazette* Staff Writer

Bazel Harrison had a root cellar. That's what Kalamazoo Valley Community College students came up with in an unscheduled archaeology course during the last two weeks.

Wednesday they began numbering and carrying away the homemade bricks that were the walls of the cellar, once a part of the home of the first permanent settler in Kalamazoo County.

The dig to find traces of the cabin began as a special three-week, between semesters course starting May 12. The class was supposed to conclude during the last week in May, but word of mouth and a May 25 story on the project in the *Gazette* caused such interest among KVCC students that a second three-week course was added by popular demand.

Paul Millikan, course instructor, said the decision to continue digging paid off. It was during the added session that the cellar was uncovered.

A brick foundation structure was found to the south of the cellar, making Millikan reasonably sure that the cabin faced either the east or west. It was the Harrison's family tradition to have the front facing a lake or other body of water, he said, so it is likely that Bazel Harrison's front door was on the west side, toward Harrison Lake.

The foundation structure is believed to have supported a hearth.

All the bricks found so far were made near the site, he added. The archaeology team found evidence of a clay pit to the south-southwest of the cabin site, near what was the Harrison Lake shoreline at the time the cabin was built in the late 1820's.

Hopefully, he said, the bricks from the root cellar can be reconstructed at the college or Kalamazoo Public Museum for display to show what remained of the first structure in Kalamazoo County.

Millikan speculated that Harrison probably built his cabin first to get immediate shelter, then cut a trap door in the floor, and began digging his root cellar some time after completion of the cabin.

The first digging session revealed a variety of artifacts, all of which will go to the museum. Included were square nails, pieces of china, part of a fireplace grate, pieces of crockery, glass and pipe stems.

The second session, with evidence drawing

students closer to the actual site, revealed the root cellar, a skeleton of a dog, a clock pendulum, a flintlock, more pipe bowls and a belt buckle.

The buried dog left some puzzling questions. Evidence was that the animal had been shot or struck in the back of the head, decapitated and buried.

Alexis Praus, director of the museum, said it was possible that the dog bit someone and was killed to get a sampling of the brain matter to see if it was rabid.

The flintlock was found in perfect condition, leading to speculation that it had been discarded in the 1830's and 40's when conversion of rifles from flintlock to percussion mechanism was popular.

The digging session on the southeast side of Harrison Lake yielded something besides artifacts.

Millikan said students have expressed interest in an informal archaeological club at KVCC. Preliminary plans are to go on test digging expeditions on Saturdays during the summer and fall.

Several people who say they know of early settler sites and Indian villages have contacted the school. At any rate, Millikan said, there are plenty of places to dig.

Kalamazoo Gazette, June 19, 1969

CHAPTER 70 - BAZEL HARRISON AND HIS INVOLVEMENT IN POLITICS

In an article written by James Stone in 1874 for the *Kalamazoo Telegraph*, he makes the following statements:

"Mr. Harrison took an active part in politics and his name is found as a delegate in nearly all of the conventions held for many years. He was an original Democrat of the 'Jackson School' and had little confidence in the opposing parties until the formation of the Republican party 'under the oaks at Jackson'. His first Republican vote was cast in 1860 for Lincoln. There are many who remember his tall, slightly bent form and flowing white beard and his clear eye when he came down from the prairie to the political meetings. During the war he read the papers with great interest with assiduity, indeed, that his eyesight was nearly destroyed. He watched the course of the contest with the liveliest interest and no one rejoiced with greater enthusiasm at the triumph of the government over its enemies."

POLITICAL MEETINGS

Referring to old copies of the Kalamazoo *Gazette*, both Nathan and his father's names appear as delegates to a number of political conventions.

The following are examples of the dates

when they participated. This information is on microfilm in the historical room of the Kalamazoo Public Library.

Saturday, September 30, 1837
    Both Nathan and Bazel with other Prairie Ronde residents were delegates. They were the following: Isaac Gould, Elias L. Stillwell, Danial Ingraham, Josiah Rosencrantz, Rose Rosencrantz, John Small, Joel Clark.

Saturday, September 30, 1837
    Meeting at House of B. Hawley in Village of Kalamazoo. Bazel and Nathan are not mentioned, but our friend Horace Comstock is listed with some of the appointed delegates: Danial B. Eldridge, Roswell Ransom, George L. Gale, Faye Aldrich, Samual Schoemacher, J. B. Henry, J. M. Cooper, Potter Eldridge, Marcus Cole. Probably the two meetings took place the same day.

Saturday, October 10, 1838
    Democratic Convention in School House of Village of Kalamazoo.

Saturday, October 19, 1839
    In Court House - Committee to examine credentials consists of Bazel Harrison, Nathan Harrison, P. McCreary, E.H. and L.J. Rosecrantz and for officers B. Harrison for Vice President - one of two S. King.

October 18, 1893

$40,000 in Gold
A Treasure Believed To Be Hidden
By the Late Dr. Bazel Harrison Near Schoolcraft
He Hoarded Gold but it Cannot be Found

One week ago last Friday, September 29, Dr. Bazel Harrison, Jr. an aged and much respected citizen of Schoolcraft, suddenly died, leaving as the result of a long life of self-denial and frugality a sum of money. The amount in dollars and cents is at this writing a matter of conjecture. Enough is known, however, regarding the habits of the deceased and remarks that had been dropped by him from time to time during the later part of his life, to make it more than a probability that his earthly possessions were of no mean order and somewhere a goodly number of yellow ducats were to be found, but--that somewhere--is still a profound mystery. The deceased has, for the past 25 years, been changing his paper and silver money into gold and those who have been most intimately connected with the affairs of the Harrisons say that the ready cash will exceed $40,000. The premises have been thoroughly searched as have every bank in this city but, as yet, nothing in the way of gold dollars has materialized. The deceased leaves one son and two daughters. His age was 79.

The home of Mr. H.G. Wells provided a refuge where James Fenimore Cooper often rested.

The people of Schoolcraft and the surrounding country for miles are much exercised over the matter and the outcome will be watched with much interest.

October 4, 1925

"Oak Openings" Material Collected by Cooper in Historic Schoolcraft Home
Famous Story of Notable Author Furnished by Pioneers of '50's, Friends of Novelist

Bearing, without doubt more historic and literary interest than any home in Kalamazoo County is the rickety brick house in Schoolcraft which at one time served as the temporary home of James Fenimore Cooper while that author was gathering material for his "Oak Openings," a story with scenes in the vicinity of the home.

Because of the fact that a great author like Cooper stopped at the home...the guest of Hezekiah G. Wells and Judge Bazel Harrison, great significance has ever since been attached to the place and visitors from far and near stop at the house annually to walk for a few brief moments over the yard in which the author once trod and to sit on the porch where Cooper often mediated of an evening.

From best information it is reported that the Wells' home was built some time between 1840 and 1850, and that Mr. Cooper visited the home early in the 50's. How long he remained at the home is not known, but the best authority has it he spent an entire summer there.

Those who have read "Oak Openings" will remember the familiar character of the Old Bee Hunter. It is claimed by Schoolcraft pioneers that Mr. Cooper depicted in the character of the Old Bee Hunter his friend and host, Judge Bazel Harrison. On the side of the house is a bronze plate with the inscription:

"AT THIS HOUSE
JAMES FENIMORE COOPER
STAYED
WHILE COLLECTING MATERIAL
FOR
OAK OPENINGS"

October 18, 1925

Hotels Were First Enterprise In City To Experience Boom
First Tavern Was Built Here in 1832; Inns of Early Days Were Rallying Point of Community

Earliest of Kalamazoo enterprises to experience a business boom were its hotels-- institutions which became the rallying places for the community and the scenes of many festive occasions in the first years of the city's history.

As early as 1834 when government land speculation was at its height travelers were moving westward in large number. There were always two persons and sometimes three in each bed. In rooms where beds could not be placed the floors were strewn with sleepers. Every house became a hostelry and pie and cake venders reaped a harvest as the hotels were unable to feed the hordes and hungry men who were turned away by the hundreds.

Built River House

Construction of the River House was started in 1834 by Nathan Harrison. In making excavations on the river bank for his hotel, workers found bones, relics and utensils which had been buried by the Indians. The discoveries included several kettles, mostly of brass, which were polished up and placed in service by the new hotel.

October 18, 1925

J. Fenimore Cooper Visited in County at Comstock Manor

James Fenimore Cooper, American novelist of Cooperstown, N.Y., made several visits to Kalamazoo County during the 40's and while here gathered the material for his story, "Oak Openings." This book describes the beauties of the Kalamazoo River and Prairie Ronde.

Together with a brother, the author owned

properties in Cooper Township, a district which still bears his family name. While here, Cooper visited at Comstock Manor, the home of General Horace H. Comstock. Mrs. Comstock was his niece and in the community also resided Mott Cooper, a nephew.

While visiting here Cooper met Bazel Harrison, the first settler of Kalamazoo County and Harrison is always credited with being the "Ben Boden" of "Oak Openings." The writer is believed to have visited here at least three times.

Correspondence of James Fenimore Cooper indicates that he did none of his writing in Kalamazoo, as has been reported. It has been established that he wrote "Oak Openings" at Cooperstown in January, 1848.

October 18, 1925

Volney Hascall joined the *Gazette* in 1834

He recites his experiences. I first visited Kalamazoo at the foot of Main Street. On the bank of the river a cabin was occupied by Nathan Harrison who operated a ferry consisting of a canoe or two and a large skiff. The day I visited the ferry, the west shore was lined with beautiful birch bark canoes of a company of Indians who had come bringing maple sugar, venison and fur pelts for trade.

About a mile below this place on the east bank of the river was an old French trading post.

Pioneer was Cooper's Hero
Schoolcraft Man Immortalized in Novel

SCHOOLCRAFT, June 19--Buried in the local cemetery is Judge Bazel Harrison, one of the most prominent pathfinders of Southwestern Michigan and the outstanding figure in the early history of Kalamazoo County. It was his personality that suggested to James Fenimore Cooper the character of Ben Boden, the bee hunter, in *Oak Openings*, the novelist's tale of the Kalamazoo valley. Harrison lived to be over 100 years old. He is believed to have arrived on Prairie Ronde November 5, 1828. At this time, Michigan Territory was an unknown country. Few had penetrated its great primeval forest or traversed its verdant prairies.

Harrison was born in Maryland, March 17, 1771. He recalled in later years how he watched six of his brothers march off to fight under Washington. Hearing stories of the beauty and fertility of Michigan, Harrison with a party of 21 set out for what they considered a land of promise in an old Pennsylvania wagon, re-sembling a huge covered boat on wheels, and several other lighter vehicles. Slowly they made their way to Fort Wayne thence to Elkhart Prairie and Baldwin's Prairie, just north of the state line. From here, Harrison, Elias Harrison, his son; Henry Whipple, his son-in-law, and

Abraham Davidson went ahead to "spy out the land."

From Indians they had learned of a large prairie 40 miles north of the Territorial line. At dusk on November 5, 1828, they lighted their campfire on the southern edge of the prairie, known to the French as Prairie Ronde, to the Indians as "Wa-we-os-co-tang-sco-tah," or "round-fire plain."

The beauty of the prairie so impressed the travelers they decided at once that they need look no farther for a more desirable place to settle. While they were eating breakfast they were visited by Chief Sagamaw and a dozen painted Indians, who welcomed them. In response to inquiries, the chief led the party to the northwest side of the prairie, where near some woods, they came to a lake known as Harrison's Lake. At that time it was much larger. Here Harrison decided to settle. That night the party camped on the edge of the lake where Harrison was to spend a half a century of his life.

Harrison erected a rude cabin and prepared to spend as comfortable a winter as was possible. The claim was entered in the government land office at Monroe. The following spring, Harrison and his sons plowed fields and planted corn and buckwheat. The seed they obtained in White Pigeon. The second year they were obliged to go to Fort Wayne for wheat and to Toland's mill, Elkhart, to have grain ground.

Harrison was the father of 17 children, the descendants of whom are widely scattered. He became one of the most dominating figures in Kalamazoo County. He was commissioned an associate judge of the county court by Governor Cass. He was a strong Democrat until 1860 when he cast his first Republican vote for Lincoln. The frame house he erected in 1831, or 1832, on the banks of the lake was destroyed by fire and replaced with another.

Harrison died August 30, 1874 and was buried September 1. Over 1,000 persons attended his funeral. The pallbearers were six of the oldest residents of the community, their combined ages being 466 years. They were John Brown, Robert Pursell, Judge E. B. Dyckman, Preston J. McCreary, Abner Mack, Godfrey Knight.

June 16, 1929

In 1833 the population grew to 100 people. John Hayes, Sr., built a house at Main and Pitcher Streets and Nathaniel Harrison started operating his ferry across the Kalamazoo River.

The first bridge was started in 1835 and was completed in 1837, putting an end to the ferry business. For the first time it was not necessary for the Detroit stage coach to plunge through the Kalamazoo River at the fording place near the Indian Trading Post.

The author stands behind the gravestone of her famous relative, Bazel Harrison, who was born in 1771 and died in 1874. He is buried in the Harrison Cemetery near Schoolcraft, Michigan.

June 16, 1929

Bazel Harrison County's First White Settler Came Here at Age of 57 and Died at Age of 103; Father of 17

Bazel Harrison, first white settler to locate in Kalamazoo County came here at the age of 57 and lived to spend 46 years in Prairie Ronde and Schoolcraft before his death August 30, 1874, at the age of 103.

Harrison became a leader in county affairs here and presided over the first court held in the county in 1831. He was the father of 17 children. John S. Harrison, youngest son, was the father of Owen, William and James Harrison and Mrs. Emma Longwell, present residents of Schoolcraft. John Harrison, now living at Climax is the son of William Harrison, first settler in Charleston Township, and Frank Harrison at Kalamazoo is the son of Ephraim Harrison, another of Bazel's sons.

The year that Bazel Harrison first arrived in Kalamazoo County has been the subject of much debate. Some contended that he arrived in 1827 and others that is was in 1828. One early historical writer set the time of his arrival as November 5, 1828.

CELEBRATE ANNIVERSARY

Despite this difference of opinion, the 100th anniversary of Harrison's arrival was officially celebrated at the home of Owen Harrison in Schoolcraft on November 27, 1927. Harrison lives on the old homestead which has has been the home of the Harrisons for more than a century. About 50 were present at the celebration in 1927 and a talk was given by Judge John W. Adams of this city.

It is estimated that the number of descendants living at various points in the country, totals about 500. A family reunion is held each year. Owen Harrison is now president of the association and the reunion this year will be held at Vicksburg on Labor Day.

Owen Harrison also has a large oil painting of Bazel Harrison made from life by Benjamin Cooley. (This is the life size one which was at the museum.)

The Harrison Homestead is located near the corner of 10th Street and U Avenue, Schoolcraft. Owen Harrison, who lived in the home in 1927, is believed to be the last of the Harrisons to dwell in the house.

June 16, 1929

Charleston Survey Made During 1926
First Settler Aided in Building Cabin by
Potawatomies

Though Charleston Township was surveyed by John Mullet in 1825 and 1826, it was not organized as a separate township until 1838. William Harrison, son of Judge Bazel Harrison, was the first settler in Charleston Township. Harrison was aided by Potawatomi Indians in erecting his cabin during the summer of 1830. He was joined by his wife, America. Harrison afterward related that without venison and food supplied by the Indians he and his small family would have starved during their first winter in Charleston.

Harrison was born in Frederick County, Virginia, January 17, 1790 and was the eldest son of Bazel Harrison.

More Settlers Arrive

Early in 1831, Asa Gunn of Washtenaw County, became the second settler of Charleston Township. Gunn was a distiller and brought a still with him. It is related, however, that in a moment of generosity, he supplied some of his product to the Indians. Their demonstrations so frightened him that he discontinued operating the still.

Public lands in Charleston were first opened to purchases in June 1831. Among the purchasers at that time were Asa Gunn, Benjamin Grenville, Horace H. Comstock, William Earl, Edwin Lothrop, Hiram Moore, Caleb Eldred, Charles Andrews, Stephan and William Eldred, James N. Fellows and Nathan Harrison.

Many other settlers came in during the next few years. In the spring of 1836, Orrin N. Giddings and John L. Cock brought in a stock of groceries and dry goods and erected a two-story frame store at what was later known as Cock's corners. The building was erected by Jesse Turner. The firm was discontinued in 1842, Cock entering business at Augusta. Giddings came to Kalamazoo after serving as the first justice of the peace and the second supervisor in Charleston.

Church and Distillery

The Methodist Church in the southwest part of the county was established in 1840 and Benjamin Hartwell opened his distillery on the Kalamazoo River at about the same time.

There is no record of the existence of a school in Charleston prior to 1837. It is said that a schoolhouse was built near the residence of Dr. James Harris in 1837. The first board of school inspectors met April 10, 1838 and organized seven school districts.

During the same summer log school houses were erected in at least four of these seven districts.

Indians Guided First Settler to New Home

Kalamazoo County's first permanent settler was guided to his Prairie Ronde homesite by Chief Sagamaw and some of his Pottowattomie braves in 1828.

Bazel Harrison, distinguished by his flowing under-chin beard, came to Kalamazoo from Ohio when he was 57 years old and lived here until his death at age 103 in 1874. He fathered 17 children, and himself was one of 23 children.

Shortly after his arrival here, Bazel was commissioned by Michigan Governor Lewis Cass as associate judge of the county court. He also served as justice of the peace.

He presided over the first court held in the county in 1831. Chronicles of the times report that he was one of the best liked men in the county by both white men and Indians. More than 1,000 persons attended his funeral on August 30, 1874 in Schoolcraft.

Bazel settled with his large family at a site on the banks of Harrison Lake in the southern part of the county. A marker near the site was placed in 1928 by the Lucinda Hinsdale Stone DAR Chapter.

The frame home of Thaddeus Smith was constructed at the edge of an oak opening in Schoolcraft in 1830.

The colorful judge also has been mentioned as the original "Bee-Hunter" character created by James Fenimore Cooper in his book, "Oak Openings."

A staunch Democrat for most of his long life, the judge shifted allegiance in 1860 when he voted for Abraham Lincoln.

June 13, 1976

Schoolcraft: Home to Early County Settlers

Schoolcraft Township is steeped in history from the "Big Island" and its association with James Fenimore Cooper to the house which served as a "stop" on the "underground railroad" of pre-Civil War days.

Early settlers were attracted to the open lands of what was originally known as "Prairie Ronde." The first doctor in the county, Dr. Nathan Thomas, reported that 60 families lived along the edges of the prairie when he arrived in 1830.

Lucius Lyon, surveyor, speculator and later U. S. Senator, platted the village of Schoolcraft in 1831. He hired a young school teacher new to the village, Stephen Vickery, to survey the streets and lots. From then through the 1860's, the village continued to grow.

The house located at 121 West Street may be one of the oldest still standing in the county. It was probably built for Thaddeus Smith about

Edna Smith, Mary Jane Swartz and Mary Crose are shown in front of the centennial maple tree planted in 1876 beside the Edna Smith home in Schoolcraft.

1833-1835. Smith first visited Prairie Ronde in 1829, spending the night with Bazel Harrison, the county's first permanent settler. He described the prairie before as "the most beautiful place in the world." He returned the next season to manage the store opened by James Smith and Hosea Huston. In 1831, according to one account, the store and one house were all that existed of Schoolcraft.

Thaddeus Smith became involved in a complicated land transaction that would end up with a farm for himself on 80 acres just east of the village boundaries and a house in the village. He farmed his land for the rest of his life and occupied his village house until his death in April 1876.

The house would remain in the Smith family hands for 100 years after that.

November 10, 1978

Calendar Turned Back on Warm, Blustery Day
Prairie Ronde...Goal at the End of a Long and
Tiring Journey through the Wilderness

by Harold T. Smith, *Gazette* Staff Writer

A sturdy wagon pulled by two teams of oxen, 21 men, women and children, dogs, a herd of cows and 50 pigs brought civilization to Kalamazoo County 150 years ago Sunday.

The tombstone of Martha Harrison, wife of Bazel Harrison, is in the Harrison Cemetery. Martha, who died on June 7, 1857 was 80 years, four months and three days old.

Prairie Ronde, a rich expanse of farmland in the southern part of the county, was their goal at the end of a long and tiring journey through the wilderness from settled Ohio and Indian lands.

They were greeted by Potawatomi Chief Sagamaw and 12 painted Indians who guided them to water on the north side of the prairie where the pioneers would make permanent homes. This scene was repeated Sunday on the prairie northwest of Schoolcraft as 450 persons gathered to commemorate the county's pioneer settlement 150 years ago to the day.

Even the warm, blustery weather Sunday was like the way it was thought to have been when the pioneer band arrived, said Alexis Praus, the master of ceremonies for the commemorative program. Praus is the retired curator of the Kalamazoo Public Museum.

"They were self-reliant, experienced and hard-working farmers...and Bazel and Martha Harrison were symbolic of those who first settled in the county," said Dr. Charles Heller, professor of geography at Western Michigan University.

Heller, Leila Carney, president of the Schoolcraft Historical Society, and U. S. Representative Garry Brown, a descendant of a prairie pioneer, spoke to the 450 who gathered for the sesquicentennial program not far from where the Harrisons settled.

From the beginning, said Heller, the pio-

BAZEL AND MARTHA HARRISON

Bazel and Martha Harrison are buried in the Harrison cemetery south of this marker. He led a party of 21 who were the first permanent settlers on Prairie Ronde Kalamazoo County, where they arrived on November 5, 1828.

One thousand people attended his funeral on September 1, 1874 because he was admired, esteemed, respected and loved by all who knew him.

Martha Stillwell Harrison died on June 7, 1857. As his wife of 67 years she shared all of his early hardships and later ease, successes and failures, joys and sorrows and was the mother of 17 children.

KALAMAZOO COUNTY SESQUICENTENNIAL COMMITTEE
November 5, 1828 – November 5, 1978

The above marker was placed at the corner of U Avenue and 10th Street at the time of the Sesquicentennial which was held November 8, 1978 in honor of the Harrisons' arrival in Prairie Ronde on November 8, 1828.

- 303 -

neers turned hundreds of acres into premier farmland.

Schoolcraft became the mart for a wide area, said Brown whose great grandfather was a partner in the county's first store.

Brown also recalled how his forebearers' Schoolcraft farm became the first agricultural research station for what would become Michigan State University.

Mrs. Carney's remarks focused on Harrison and his wife who headed the first group of settlers here. Prairie Ronde proved fruitful for them, she said. Martha Harrison lived to be 83 and Bazel Harrison lived to be 103.

Among the participants in Sunday's program were the Harrisons' descendants who are scattered in several communities across southern Michigan.

A county historical marker to note the Harrison settlement and burial sites was unveiled Sunday at the corner of U Avenue and 10th Street, just east of the Harrison settlement site at Harrison Lake.

The prairie program was the first of several planned to coincide with the 150th anniversary of the settlement of Bronson (Kalamazoo) in 1829, the creation of the county by territorial governor in 1829, the formal organization of the county in 1830 and settlement of other communities in the county in 1830. In connection with the sesquicentennial, the Kalamazoo Public Museum in downtown Kala-

*The photograph of Judge Harrison was taken from a
painting done by Anthony Cooley in 1867.*

mazoo has set up a display of artifacts found at the Harrison settlement site by archaeology students a few years ago. The museum's display will be open to the public during November.

September 25, 1990

Historical Portrait Get Face Lift

by Mark Maher, *Kalamazoo Gazette* Reviewer

Kalamazoo's first permanent settler, Bazel Harrison, has been given new life...or at least his portrait has!

Kalamazoo Public Museum Curator of Collections Ellen Penwell reports that the portrait of Harrison, done in 1867 by local artist Benjamin Cooley recently went through a complex cleaning and mending process and has been restored to immaculate condition.

Penwell comments: "The results are just remarkable. Visitors will enjoy seeing what an interesting portrait it truly is." The Harrison portrait is part of a museum exhibit titled "Faces of Kalamazoo" featuring paintings of Kalamazooans from the museum's permanent collection. The show ran from September, 1990 through January, 1991.

The Kalamazoo County Court House, which was erected in 1887, was the home of the painting of Judge Bazel Harrison for about 50 years. This is a 1910 photo.

EPILOGUE

As this book comes to a conclusion, let us refer to two people who are well qualified to give their evaluation of the life of Judge Bazel Harrison.

First we will open the book of *Oak Openings* to page 240 where James Fenimore Cooper sums up in a few words the attributes of the one who he used as a prototype for his Ben Boden.

"On one side of this island of wood lies the little village, or large hamlet of Schoolcraft. Here we were most cordially welcomed by General Boden, and all of his fine descendants. The head of this family is approaching seventy, but is still hale and hearty. His head is as white as snow, and his face as red as a cherry. A finer old man one seldom sees. Temperance, activity, the open air and a good conscience, have left him a noble ruin; if ruin he can yet be called. He owes the last blessing, as he told us himself, to the fact that he kept clear of the whirlwind of speculation that passed over this region some ten or fifteen years since. His means are ample, and the harvest being about to commence, he invited me to the field."

Secondly, we will now turn to pages 29, 30 and 31 of the book *A Biographical Sketch of Judge Bazel Harrison*, by James H. Stone, in which he makes a number of memorable statements. They are as follows;

"Grand old centenarian, around his long

and eventful life how many associations cluster! In the hundred years of his life the grandest scenes in the history of the world have been enacted, the brightest pages of progress have been written, the noblest men have fulfilled their missions and passed away. Far beyond the time allotted to man's life, he has lived to see his children grow to old age, and his children's children filling useful positions in the world. His days have been full of comfort and enjoyment, his lines have been cast in pleasant places, and peace, like a beautiful halo, settled around the lingering sunset of his life. Patiently, and with full confidence in the sublime promises of Him who created worlds and time and man, he awaited the welcome summons for this mortal to put on immortality, to renew his youth in the fountains of Eternal Life, and at last passed away.

Like one
Who wraps the drapery of his couch about him and lies down to pleasant dreams!"

THE LAST SAD RITES

The funeral of Judge Harrison took place Tuesday afternoon, September 2, 1874, from the residence of his son, John S. Harrison, situated near the little lake where the deceased first settled forty-six years ago. The attendance was very large, nearly every family on Prairie Ronde and Gourdneck Prairie being represented, so that probably not less than eight hundred persons were present to show this last mark of respect to the revered dead. The exercises were very simple and conducted by Rev. T. Mills, of Calhoun County, who formerly preached on Prairie Ronde and officiated at the funeral of the Judge's wife seventeen years ago.

Five of the eight surviving children were present: William, Nathan, Bazel, Jr., John S., and Mrs. Almira Harrison Crose. Nathan, better known as the "River Ferryman" of Kalamazoo forty years ago, the second surviving son who is now 78 years old, arrived from his home in Bloomfield, Wisconsin, during the services. Mrs. Cynthia Harrison Whipple, Mrs. Worlenda Harrison Fellows and Mrs. Martha Harrison Bishop, the other surviving children were not present. The two first named live in Minnesota, and Mrs. Bishop's home is Fairwater, Wisconsin.

The following grandchildren were present: Jeremiah Harrison (and wife), Joseph Harrison (and wife), and John Harrison, sons of William the oldest son; Hattie Harrison Vanduzer (and husband), George Harrison (and wife), John S. Harrison and Mary L. Harrison, children of Bazel Harrison, Jr.; George Crose (and wife), William Crose (and wife), Dayton Crose (and wife), Jesse Crose (and wife), children of Almira Harrison Crose; William Harrison (and wife), Esther, James, Sarah and Emma Harrison, children of John S. Harrison, youngest son of the deceased. There were also seven great-grandchildren present, and a considerable number of family relatives who were not descendants.

The six pall bearers were John Brown, who settled on Prairie Ronde in 1830; P. J. McCreary, who came the same year; Godfrey Knight and Abram Mack, who came in 1832; E. B. Dyckman, who came in 1836; and Robert Pursell, who settled in Schoolcraft in 1844. The oldest of the bearers was 84, and the youngest 69, and the aggregate ages of the six was 466 years. It was an affecting scene as the aged bearers bore the casket containing the remains of the centenarian from the house to the hearse, and at the grave tenderly lowered it to its last resting place, and none of the hundreds who were present will ever forget it."

BIBLIOGRAPHY

Burten, Dwight, *The History of the Schoolcraft United Methodist Church, 1832-1982.*

Cooper, James Fenimore, *Oak Openings.* New York: P. F. Collier, 1892

Dunbar, Willis, *Kalamazoo and How it Grew.* Kalamazoo, Michigan: Western Michigan University School of Graduate Studies, 1951.

Hampton, Charles F., *Michigan Log Cabins and Hard Cider.* Brighton, Michigan: Green Oak Press, 1984

Kalamazoo Public Library Pioneer Collection. *History of Kalamazoo County, Michigan*

Massie, Larry B., *From Frontier Folk to Factory Smoke.* Au Train, Michigan: Avery Color Studios, 1987

Massie, Larry B., and Peter Schmitt. *Kalamazoo, The Place Behind the Products, An Illustrated History,* 1981.

Michigan Pioneer Collections. 40 Vols. 1877-1929.

Pitcher, Emma B., "Prairie Grass is in Full Bloom", Kalamazoo Gazette. Sept. 17, 1989. Section E-1.

Potts, Grace. *Kalamazoo Long Ago.* Kalamazoo, Michigan: Ihling Brothers. 1955

Schmitt, Peter & Balthazar Korab. Kalamazoo. *Nineteenth Century Homes in a Midwestern Village.* The Kalamazoo Historical Commission. 1976.

Schmidt, Wayne. *The Vanishing Prairie*. Kalamazoo Gazette, January 11, 1987.

Sloane, Eric. *Diary of an Early American Boy, Noah Blake, 1805*. New York: Wilfred Funk, Inc. 1962.

Stone, James H. *A Biographical Sketch of Judge Bazel Harrison, The First White Settler in Kalamazoo County, 1874*.

Swartz, Mary Jane. *So I'm Told. The Nineteenth Century in Schoolcraft, Michigan*. Berrien Springs, Michigan: Hardscrabble Books, 1989.

The One Room Schools of Greenfield Village, Information and ideas for teachers. Detroit, Michigan.

The Reader's Digest Association, Pleasantville, New York. *The Story of America*, 1975

World Book Encylopedia, Volume 16. *The Erie Canal*, 1958.

Index

THE AUTHOR

Mary Elizabeth Crose was born in Montpelier, Ohio. When she was four years old, her family moved to Kalamazoo, Michigan, where she spent most of her life. She attended Kalamazoo Public Schools and Western Michigan University, where she earned a BA degree.

After completing four years of college, she continued to take undergraduate courses, one of which stimulated her to tutor children with disabilities in the basic school subjects. She tutored full time for ten years, mostly under the supervision of the Kalamazoo Child Guidance Center.

In 1950 a need arose in the Kalamazoo Public Schools for a resource room involving visually impaired students. Miss Crose was asked to pursue training in this field of education. She spent nine months preparing for this pioneer work at Perkins Institute for the Visually Impaired located at Watertown, Massachusetts, which offered a course which was affiliated with Harvard University. Miss Crose completed this training and stayed in the east for a summer session at the Boston Nursery Training School.

During the spring vacation she attended a conference in New York, which was offered to teachers engaged in dealing with visually impaired babies and young children.

She began her work at the Parkwood Upjohn School in September of 1952 and continued in this capacity until June of 1964 when the Kalamazoo Public Schools decided to build the John F. Kennedy Center for the Mentally Impaired. Again, she was asked to pioneer in this new endeavor. Six years later she retired.

In addition to teaching, Miss Crose became a "mother" to several homeless children. She was a Red Cross Volunteer for 30 years, serving as a teacher-sponsor for 15 years and at Friendship Village another 15. She taught both Sunday School and Junior Church for many years as well.

In September of 1976 she moved into Friendship Village where she is still actively involved.